Millersburg Glass
As I Know It

MARIE McGEE

edited by
James Measell

photography by
David Richardson

The Glass Press, Inc.
dba Antique Publications
Post Office Box 553 • Marietta, Ohio 45750

PB ISBN #1-57080-005-7   HB ISBN #1-57080-006-7

Dedication

**This book is dedicated to Don Doyle,
who likes Millersburg glass as much as I do, *almost!*
And to Frank M. Fenton, who has given so much of his time
in answering collectors' questions
on everything
relating to glass.**

FRONT COVER

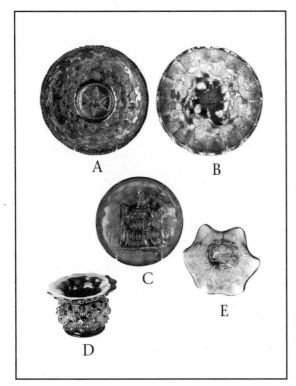

BACK COVER

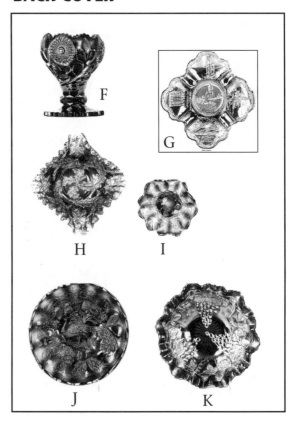

A.   Green Carnival Many Stars ice cream
      bowl (note radium finish)

B.   Marigold Carnival Strawberry
      Wreath ice cream bowl

C.   Amethyst Carnival Millersburg Court
      House 7" ice cream shape bowl
      (note radium finish)

D.   Amethyst Carnival Swirl Hobnail
      spittoon

E.   Blue Carnival Millersburg Peacock
      6" ruffled sauce dish

F.   Green Carnival Hobstar and Feather
      rose bowl

G.   Amethyst Carnival Cleveland Memorial
      ashtray

H.   Vaseline Carnival Whirling Leaves
      square bowl

I.   Amethyst Carnival Strawberry Wreath
      6" flat sauce dish

J.   Amethyst Carnival Peacock
      ice cream bowl

K.   Blue Carnival Vintage 10" bowl
      with Hobnail back

CONTENTS

Why did I ever think I could write a book? When this project started, I wasn't sure I could. There is so much information that needs to be shared. The encouragement and help from collectors, friends and family has given me the incentive and motivation to try.

The characteristic iridescence of Carnival glass with its array of rainbow colors has always interested me, but the glass made by Millersburg was my first choice, and it has continued. My interest in Millersburg's crystal glass developed much later. When I started putting together a collection, very little information was available about Millersburg glass. The comment I often heard from some early collectors was as follows: "I don't really care for it, and the finish looks like new glass." That opinion has changed!

I purchased the books by Marion Hartung and Rose Presznick as well as any book on Carnival glass that was available. When Bill Edwards' *Millersburg Queen of Carnival Glass* was published, it became my most valued reference, and its photographs enabled me to recognize patterns.

O. Joe Olson was one of the first with whom I corresponded and talked about Millersburg. I was invited to his home in Kansas City where I first saw some very rare examples of Millersburg which are still in demand now.

Living on the West coast, I had less opportunity to see the famous collections, but I was fortunate to share "one on one" learning with Sherman Hand and Don Moore. They were among the first researchers, and Don Moore was most knowledgeable on all glass. Don and Connie Moore shared their collection with everyone at their home and at conventions. C. B. (Bill) Carroll probably owned every Millersburg pattern and shape known at one time or another, and he was always willing to answer questions. Charlotte Williams, Marie Capps and Ed Garner were also a big help in my early learning.

Jack and Liz Wilson's Millersburg "Research Notes" and all the Carnival glass club newsletters were good sources of information. The Lincoln-Land newsletter is a good source for research on Millersburg glass. Don Doyle has helped with this research. It would take pages to name all the collectors who responded and shared information on my questionnaires. My sincere thanks to each of you.

The purpose of this publication is education and information, whether collecting, buying or selling. Most of all, I hope to keep collecting interesting as a hobby so people will continue to collect and treasure the rare and beautiful American glass made at Millersburg.

Marie McGee
3906 E. Acacia Ave.
Fresno, CA 93726-0907

January, 1995

```
┌─────────────────┬──────────────────────────────┬──────────────────┐
│                 │  MILLERSBURG GLASS CO.,       │  TEA SETS        │
│ ALL THE LATEST  │  ⇝ MANUFACTURERS OF ⇜         │      WATER SETS  │
│ NOVELTIES IN GLASS │ Plain and Decorated Glassware │ LEMONADE SETS   │
│                 │                              │      BERRY SETS  │
└─────────────────┴──────────────────────────────┴──────────────────┘
```

MILLERSBURG, OHIO,

Acknowledgments

My sincere thanks to the following people who sent pictures and allowed their beautiful items to be photographed for this book. Without you, my desire to show the beauty of Millersburg Carnival glass could not have been accomplished. The generosity of sharing glass and knowledge is an important part of collecting.

Jack and Mary Adams
Elden and Juanita Bicksler
Richard and Bonnie Boldt
James and Marie Capps
David and Libby Cotton
Jerry and Carol Curtis
Robert and Patricia Davis
Don Doyle
Frank M. Fenton
Sam Finney
Dean and Diane Fry

Bob Grissom
Richard and Merri Houghton
Bob and Geneva Leonard
Steve and Heather Maag
Judy Maxwell
Eugene and Shirley Metro
David and Joyce Middleton
Charles and Eleanor Mochel
Bill and Carol Richards
Edward and Barbara Stalder
Floyd and Cecil Whitley

Very special thanks go to Dave and Joan Doty (who did some photography for me) and to my typist, Eileen Betts.

Lucille Lowe and George Irving also deserve recognition for their efforts to preserve the history of Millersburg glass.

BY JAMES MEASELL, DIRECTOR OF GLASS HISTORY RESEARCH, ANTIQUE PUBLICATIONS

For a brief period, the town of Millersburg, Ohio, was the focus of the American glass tableware industry.

Drawing upon investors from Marietta, Ohio, erstwhile promotor and glassman John W. Fenton masterminded the construction of the Millersburg Glass Company. The Hipkins Novelty Mould Company of Martins Ferry, Ohio—one of the best such shops in the United States—was engaged to make the first moulds.

The Millersburg firm's initial products—pressed crystal items in imitation of cut glass made in 1909—soon gave way to vivid, dazzling iridescent articles made by spraying the still-hot glass with liquid solutions of metallic salts. Today, glass collectors call this "Carnival glass." This glassware has been a mainstay on the American antiques scene for decades, and it is not an exaggeration to say that American Carnival glass, including Millersburg's distinctive patterns, is now known worldwide.

Throughout 1910, John Fenton's Millersburg wares competed with the similar iridescent lines being made by the Northwood, Dugan and Imperial enterprises as well as those originated by John's brother, Frank L. Fenton, at the Fenton Art Glass Company in Williamstown, West Virginia.

The Millersburg plant quickly added patterns and novelty articles to its repertoire as John Fenton and others called upon their talents as glass designers to win the public's fancy. For a time, they were successful. In 1911, the bubble burst, and the Millersburg Glass Company went into a financial tailspin.

The plant was put into operation once more as the Radium Glass Company with John Fenton again at the helm, backed by new investors. Seeking to recapture its reputation for innovative iridescent ware, the venture flourished for just a short time before falling idle forever in May, 1912.

Now, well-known Millersburg glass collector Marie McGee has completed this long-awaited project, and she tells the full story of Millersburg glass, especially Millersburg's Carnival glass. Patterns made at Millersburg are carefully documented and detailed. Rare and unusual colors are discussed. A chronological account of the Millersburg glass plants and John Fenton's role in them has been developed for those readers who revel in historical details.

This postcard shows the Millersburg Glass Company plant about the time it began operations.

Millersburg, Ohio — Glass Co.

Pub. by G. U. Duer.

Glossary

Terms Used for Patterns and Shapes

Due to the many variations and shapes in the Carnival glass patterns and items made by Millersburg, it's important to learn to identify and to know terms used to describe these articles. Sometimes there are vast differences in value, desirability, or availability in the same patterns and/or sizes—with seemingly minor variations making all the difference! Collectors have coined many terms in their attempts to simplify confusion.

Bowls are known in more variations and shapes than other item. Not all bowls were made for use in the typical berry sets consisting of a large bowl and six smaller ones. Such sets are now extremely rare, and complete sets exist in Carnival glass for only a few patterns. Bowls were originally listed as "nappies" but they are called bowls and **sauce dishes** now. The sauce dishes are generally scarce and are some of the most desirable pieces of Carnival glass.

Individual bowls are known in various shapes with either **collar bases** or **domed bases** [editor's note: originally, glassworkers used the term "marie" for collar base and the term "foot" for domed base]. These bowls, especially the larger ones, come with different edges. A simple **scalloped edge** may have been imparted by the mould itself. Other bowls were subjected to finishing operations to make them **six-ruffled** or **crimped** in various ways, including the attractive **candy ribbon edge** or the **three-in-one edge**. All of these bowls were originally intended as fruit bowls. The candy ribbon edge takes its name from the distinctive symmetrical shape of the confection, while the three-in-one edge has two smaller indentations followed by a larger one.

The large berry bowls measure 8" to 9" in diameter and are about 3" to 4" deep. The smaller sauce dishes are 5" to 6" diameter. The deep, scalloped edge style is very popular in both large and small bowls, but a complete set is extremely rare. The shallow bowl with six-ruffles and a candy ribbon edge is also known, but rarely found, in complete sets.

The **ice cream bowl** is a round unruffled bowl with collar base that is quite flat although the edges turn up sharply. A true ice cream master bowl usually measures about 10" in diameter, but such Millersburg bowls may measure from 9 1/4" to 10" or slightly more. Bowls of smaller size are also described as the ice cream shape. Bowls 5" to 6" in diameter were certainly made for sets, but very few seem to have survived, and complete sets are rarely seen.

The term **Variant** is applied to an example that differs slightly in form from the standard version of a particular item. Sometimes the differences are quite minor, such as the presence or absence of a small detail in the design or a change in size due to the way a piece was finished by the glassmaker. Several Variants are discussed later in this book.

The "**Mystery**" Peacock and Urn Millersburg bowl is no longer a real mystery, of course, but this name has allowed the overused word "Variant" to be put aside. The Mystery Peacock and Urn bowl can be identified by the two rows of beading on the urn and a much larger bee. Measurements are 8 3/4" to 9" in diameter; most of these have the three-in-one edge, although a few ice cream shapes are known.

Shotgun is the name collectors often use for the Millersburg 7" Peacock and Urn bowl which was labeled earlier as a Variant. There is no urn and no beading, but the bowl does have the typical bee.

Tendrils are slender, coiling stemlike parts by which a climbing plant attaches itself to a support. This definition comes from *Webster's New Riverside Dictionary*. This term is often used in describing aspects of Millersburg's Wreath patterns. The tendrils enhance the beauty of the art work and designs.

A **whimsey** is a creative expression which departs from the normal example. Whim is defined as a sudden unexpected notion or a fanciful idea. The hot glass is re-shaped or finished after it comes out of the mould. About 1909, these were called "stunts" in the glass trade. A swung vase made from a spooner mould is a good example of a stunt. Carnival glass collectors use the word whimsey to describe changes in shape. Whimseys can be one of a kind or with only a few known. All are highly desirable and considered very rare. Moulds for rose bowls, spittoons and spooners were often used. Bowls were also used. Since plates are so rare, it's probable they were made as bowls and re-shaped by flattening. Some examples could have been experimental or for promotional use.

Terms Used in Glassmaking

Cullet is leftover or broken glass. Sometimes this glass would be saved to be re-melted in later batches of glass. Early glass plants often disposed of broken glass by simply putting it on a scrap heap on the plant grounds. Lucille Lowe and George Irving were able to examine a large amount of cullet from the Millersburg plant site, and much of the information they gained was shared with Sherman Hand. Lucille Lowe's grandson, David Hall, is continuing this important research.

Plunger: The mould produces the pattern on the outside surface (exterior or back or secondary pattern), while the plunger creates the inside (interior or primary) pattern as it presses the molten glass against the mould. Many examples have both interior and exterior patterns. Plungers are of standard sizes, so they could be used with more than one mould to create combinations with a variety of different interior patterns. On Millersburg this is found in many of the patterns.

Proof is a term that Carnival glass collectors use to describe what they believe is a trial impression from a plunger/mould combination. Two examples are the Strawberry Wreath with an unfinished leaf (only the outline) and the Peacock Whimsey Proof, where a section of one leg on the Peacock is missing. Both Strawberry Wreath and Peacock are interior patterns, so they are made by the plunger. The pattern must be chipped into the plunger so that it will stand out in low relief from the surface of the glass after pressing. The areas in question on these specimens likely occur because the pattern was left incomplete, probably inadvertently so, on a complex design. After making some pieces, the glassworkers might notice the incomplete areas, and the plunger could go back to the mould shop to be completed.

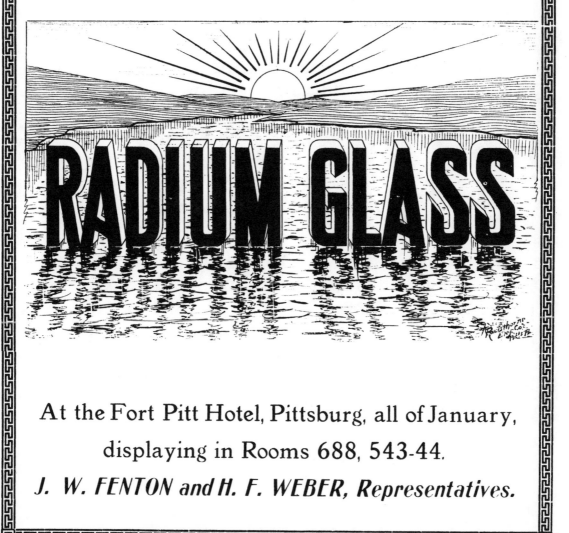

The
MILLERSBURG GLASS CO.,

Millersburg, Ohio,

Creators of *New* and *Exclusive* things in

GLASSWARE

RADIUM GLASS

At the Fort Pitt Hotel, Pittsburg, all of January, displaying in Rooms 688, 543-44.

J. W. FENTON and H. F. WEBER, Representatives.

From *China, Glass and Lamps*, January 15, 1910.

Iridescent glass is achieved by spraying the still-hot pressed glass with a solution containg metallic salts such as ferric (iron) chloride or stannous (tin) chloride. The temperature of the glass was important, as this observation reveals: "Spray on glass very hot for Matt Iridescence and not so hot for Bright Iridescence" (quoted from p. 61 of *Harry Northwood: The Wheeling Years,1901-1925*, by William Heacock, James Measell and Berry Wiggins). The **radium** finish so prized by Millersburg Carnival glass collectors, Frank M. Fenton believes, may be that "Bright Iridescence" technique described above. Many Millersburg pieces display a **satin** finish, which is quite attractive but not as bright as the radium finish.

Lustred ware is also a kind of iridescent glass. It was not made by spraying hot glass, and little is known about its history during Millersburg's time. Lustred ware is a kind of hand-decorated glass, produced by using a brush to apply metallic salt solutions to glass which has been annealed and cooled to room temperature. The glass is then placed in a decorating lehr, and the heat therein results in an iridescent effect much like the glassware that was sprayed while hot. This method was probably tried at Millersburg but found to be more labor-intensive (and thus more expensive) than spraying hot glass. The spraying method may also have produced more desirable iridescent effects, such as Millersburg's Radium ware, than could be had with lustred ware.

Vaseline is a name that was not then applied to the glass colors being made during the time of the Millersburg plants. This type of glass, made by using uranium-containing compounds in the batch, was known by various names, such as canary, yellow, topaz, and yellow-green. In 1938, a Fenton Art Glass Company catalog used the term vaseline, and the name was generally popular among glass collectors by the 1950s.

Millersburg's Vaseline has a definite yellowish-greenish tint and will "glow" under black light. The high cost of production could have been the reason for the very few examples known from the short time of glassmaking in Millersburg. Vaseline is identified by using an ultraviolet light known as a black light. In books on "Vaseline glass," there is nothing written about Millersburg's glass of this type.

CHAPTER ONE

Millersburg's Crystal Glass

In the early days of glassmaking in Millersburg, crystal glass was the first product. A short time later, colored iridescent glass was made, probably with formulas and techniques similar to those used at the Fenton glass factory in Williamstown, West Virginia. The first Millersburg crystal patterns in mid-1909 were probably the Ohio Star and the Hobstar and Feather motifs, both of which were likely designed by John W. Fenton. By October, 1909, Hobstar and Feather items (cracker jar, pitcher and tumbler) began to appear in Butler Brothers catalogs.

In a Butler Brothers wholesale catalog for Fall, 1910, Millersburg crystal patterns and shapes were listed as "Brilliant Star Jeweled Panel Design" and featured as the "New Pacemaker Assortment." No original Millersburg pattern names or numbers were given by Butler Brothers, just descriptions and sizes. Several patterns were given descriptive names, but not the ones we know today; for example, Hobstar and Feather was called "sunflower and leaf." The pitchers listed in the "Marathon" jug assortment were the Feather and Heart and the Marilyn, and they were described as "deep daisy and fan" and "feather and star cutting," respectively. The old wholesale prices from the early catalogs are fun to read!

Patterns by Millersburg shown in various Butler Brothers catalogs include Ohio Star (vases and the tall compote). Many pieces of Hobstar and Feather were shown: berry bowls; celery boats; flared salad bowls; a 10" x 7" table dish; footed jelly dish; large pitcher (called Mammoth); covered sugar; spooner; the giant rose bowl; and a large punch set, complete with cups.

Two pieces of the Potpourri pattern were shown, the high footed salver and a fruit bowl. Millersburg secondary patterns in a Butler Brothers "Mighty Bargain" bowl assortment are Fine Cut and Heart, Cactus, and Mayflower. In a Butler Brothers "New Pacemaker Assortment," there are two bowls that have a secondary pattern which was hard to identify; it's the Near-Cut Wreath on the exterior of the Holly Sprig and Holly Whirl bowls.

Some Millersburg moulds that weren't sold for scrap metal may have been acquired by the Jefferson firm, which had a factory in Canada. The Wild Rose Lamp moulds were modified at some time to add the "Riverside" name. Some crystal found in Millersburg patterns isn't as heavy and doesn't have the clarity or brilliance that most Millersburg-made examples seem to have.

My interest in crystal glassware started much later than with the iridescent colored Carnival glass. The first thoughts of it as a collector's item for me started with the Jack Wilson auction in 1982. My interest increased after Bill Edwards' *Millersburg Crystal Glassware* was published in 1982.

The purpose of this chapter is to update some earlier material and to share my experiences as a collector, based upon the Millers-

Millersburg crystal from Butler Brothers catalogs, 1909–1912.

◆◆ **HIGH FOOTED SALVER AND FRUIT BOWL ASST.—(Crystal)** ◆◆

Excellent patterns—Items that sell every day in the year.   Unmatchable at this price.

1C1567 — Good crystal, brilliant star and jeweled panel design, fire polish. Comprises: 2 doz. footed bowls, diam. 7½, round and crimped shapes. 1 doz. 9 in. cake salvers. Total 3 doz. in bbl. 112 lbs. **Doz. 92c**

"Variety Design" Bonbon Dishes.

1C460—4 shapes—diamond, club, heart, spade, about 5 in. diam., crystal, sunburst medallions within leaf wreaths. 1 doz. in box, asstd............ ....Doz. **39c**

"MAMMOTH" GLASS PITCHER.

Extra size —new striking design —low priced.

1C586 — Mammoth low shape, ht. 8, girth 22½, capacity 3½ qts., extra heavy sparkling crystal, massive sunburst and leaf panel base, plain top. 1 pkg. **Each, 35c**

"EXTRA LARGE" NEW DESIGN CRYSTAL FLOWER VASE.

Rich attractive mold, distinct new design.

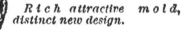

1C587—Ht. 9 in., diam. 7 in cupped mammoth flower, mold, scallop top extra heavy fine crystal, prominent deep cut sunflower and serpentine leaf design, flaring sunflower cut base. 1 in pkg. **Each, 33c**

"PRESCUT" HIGH FOOTED COMPORT ASSORTMENT.

A popular item in this high grade Prescut glass.

1C1760—Diam. about 6¼ in., round shape on fancy colonial stem foot, ht. 7½ in., 1½ doz. each of the 2 rich deep cut designs as illustrated, both brilliantly finished and fire polished. 3 doz. in bbl. 81 lbs.

Per dozen, 95c

"MASSIVE" COVERED CRACKER JAR.

1C585 —Mammoth covered shapes, 6¾ x 6¾, extra heavy brilliant finish crystal, deep cut sunburst and encircling leaf design. 1 in pkg....... ....**Each, 33c**

"PACEMAKER" GLASSWARE ASSORTMENT.

12 bouncing bargains. The smallest is excellent 10c value, majority are 25 centers. Prompt ordering is necessary as demand will be large.

1C1568: Mammoth sizes, brilliant patterns, fire polished heavy crystal.

⅙ doz. 8½ in. footed deep comport.	⅙ doz. 10¼x7 celery or table dish.
½ " heavy cream pitcher, ht. 4¼.	½ " 6¾ in. deep nut bowl.
½ " spoonholder.	½ " 9 in. high footed salver.
⅓ " covered sugar bowl.	½ " 8¾ in. flared salad.
⅙ " massive covered butter.	¼ " 7¼ in. footed deep bowl.
½ " 8 in. deep round berry bowl, 6 doz. in bbl.	⅙ " 9½ in. flared fruit bowl.

Per dozen, **86c**

"MAGNIFICENT" TABLE SET ASST.

1C1709—1 Colonial, 3 neat cut patterns, extra heavy best crystal, full finished. 3 sets each. 12 sets in bbl. 100 lbs.

Set, **33c**

"NEW PACEMAKER" ASSORTMENT. (Crystal)
Bigger and better than any ever before offered at this price.

1C1592: Extra heavy, deep cut pattern, best crystal, full finished, asst. comprises:

½ doz. 10 in. vase.	½ doz. 8 in. high footed fruit bowl.	½ doz. 10 in. flared salad bowl.
½ " 9 " berry bowl.	½ doz. 10x7 in. table dish.	½ doz. ½ gal. pitcher.
½ " 10 " celery boat.	½ " 5¾ in. footed jelly dish.	½ doz. 8¼ in. high footed fruit comport.
½ " 7 " deep nut bowl.		
½ " ½ gal. jug.	Total 6 doz. in tierce,	lbs.
½ " 8 in. berry bowl.		

Doz. **89c**

"MARATHON" JUG ASST.
The kind that has always jobbed at $2.00 dozen.

C2121: 2 styles, full finished crystal, so called ½ gal., 8¼ in. tall, 1½ doz. each deep daisy and fan, and feather and star cutting. 3 doz. tierce.

Doz. **$1.10**

burg crystal patterns in my collection, examples I have seen, and some that have been reported to me.

One of the most interesting research projects involved what previously has been thought to be the Millersburg Diamonds pattern in crystal with the ruby-stain that some call "flashing." As it turns out, these pieces are not Millersburg at all! They were made at a glass plant in Tarentum, Pa., and the pattern was called "Manhattan" in the late 1890s, about a decade before the Millersburg plant even existed!

Another research project focused on a ruby-stained "Button Arches" pattern toothpick holder which is inscribed "Millersburg Carnival Glass, Millersburg, Ohio Founded 1909." These were made at the Guernsey Glass Co. in Cambridge, Ohio, for Lucille Lowe, who sold them in conjunction with one of the Millersburg-Holmes County antique festivals in the early 1970s.

There seems to be a renewed interest in Millersburg crystal. The increases in asking prices and collectors' desire for both crystal and iridescent glass has enabled Millersburg crystal to become a popular collectible item.

PATTERNS AND SHAPES IN MILLERSBURG CRYSTAL

Cactus

The 9" bowl is best-known; the pattern is on the exterior, and it is also found as an exterior pattern on the iridescent Rays and Ribbons bowl. Some of the Cactus bowls aren't as clear or the quality of glass isn't as good as some other examples, but the beauty of the pattern as seen through the crystal makes up for it. You don't see too many of these around.

Country Kitchen

This pattern, also an exterior motif, is found in both crystal and some examples in Carnival glass. It is also the exterior pattern on Fleur de Lis. It is interesting with a pleasing combination of several designs. With the center star showing through the clear crystal, it looks like the center of a beautiful flower. Some examples—such as table set pieces and advertising bowls or plates—are extremely rare.

Advertising bowl. About 8" in diameter, this was probably made with the same mould that was used for the plate. It reads as follows: "Compliments of Illinois Furniture Company. Honest Values, 3609 Halsted St."

Advertising plate. About 9" in diameter, this one says only "Compliments of Bijou Theatre," and it's rare and desirable. The flat plate is also known with no advertising. Other sizes (5", 7", 10" and 12") have been reported, too.

Bowls. These plain items range from 5" (sauce dish) to 9" diameter. The larger ones are fairly deep compared to other berry bowls. Some 5" sauce dishes are pulled in at the top and look like a small rose bowl. The 10" ice cream bowl is shallow and shows the design well, making it a desirable item.

Table set. The complete set—covered butterdish, covered sugar bowl, creamer and spooner—has been reported, although I have not seen them yet.

Country Kitchen Variant (Opalescent)

This round, gently ruffled bowl is 7 1/2" diameter and 2 3/4" deep. My favorite words, "rare" and "desirable," were the only words I could use when I saw this example of a Country Kitchen crystal bowl with an opalescent edge. Another bowl, made from a different mould, is almost square with a distinct shape accomplished by hand-finishing.

Diamonds

For many years, this was considered to be one of Millersburg's rare crystal patterns that was occasionally found with ruby-stain decoration. I have always wondered why the design in crystal is different from the Diamonds in iridescent Carnival glass.

Now, the answer is known. Many of these pieces were actually made about 1898 at the Tarentum Glass Co. in Tarentum, Pa.! The Tarentum plant called the pattern Manhattan, and it was advertised in a T. M. Roberts Co. catalog that is shown in William Heacock's *Ruby-Stained Glass from A to Z* (p. 239). Collectors should study this catalog excerpt carefully. Based on this evidence, the table set articles and other items previously attributed to Millersburg must be re-evaluated. They are nice American-made pattern glass, but they are not Millersburg!

The crystal Diamonds compote shown in Edwards' *Millersburg Crystal Glassware* (p. 21) appears to be the same article as the one in Carnival glass which does double duty as the base for the punch bowl. The "banana boat" Edwards pictures (p. 20) is hard to discern; it could be Millersburg's Diamonds, but it's probably another instance of Tarentum's Manhattan pattern instead.

Feather and Heart

This is another of the imitation cut designs; it's heavy, brilliant crystal. The pitcher was shown in a Butler Brothers' catalog in 1910, and a tumbler has been reported.

Fine Cut Heart

The bowl is 10" in diameter and 3" deep, Fine Cut Heart is an exterior pattern on iridescent Primrose bowls. This was shown in a 1910 Butler Brothers catalog which described it as "full finished crystal." The pattern showing through the crystal is very pretty. I was happy to add this one to my collection, and I don't believe there are very many of these to be found.

Hanging Cherries

The water pitcher is the lone item reported.

Hobstar and Feather

This pattern and Ohio Star were probably designed by John W. Fenton and were the first glass made in May, 1909. Mould drawings dated in April, 1909, show several different items.

On most of the Hobstar and Feather pieces, a plain round indented circle is found in the center of the hobstar. On other pieces, there is a decorative gemstone cut hobnail that has a tiny star in its center. Years ago, some collectors believed these differences would separate Millersburg glass from Jefferson glass. Since both designs are found on Carnival glass, I find this hard to believe.

The factory's pattern No. 358, Hobstar and Feather, was described as "top quality crystal" in the glass trade publications. Many shapes and sizes were made, all in useful items for the home. These are listed below, using today's popular names for them.

Applesauce boat. This is nice clear crystal, but with feathers found in both clear and frosted. It measures 4" wide by 8" long and it is shaped much like a banana dish.

Banana boat. Quite a beauty, this measures 11" in length and is turned up quite high. These aren't easy to find.

Berry set. The large bowl is 9" in diameter and 3" deep. The small bowl is about 5" in diameter, but there are some detail differences found in these small bowls.

When I saw the hobstar's center, it is prismatic with a definite little star. I looked at every Hobstar and Feather, and I found this center only on these bowls and on the amethyst square bowl and amethyst 5" sauce dish.

Bridge set. The complete four-piece set is made up of spade, club, heart and diamond shapes. These could be small mint dishes, and they are very rare. I have only seen two (the heart and diamond shapes), but complete sets are reported.

Celery boat. This was reported to me as 10" long, 4 3/4" across, and 2 1/2" deep. I have seen a deeper oval bowl, about the same shape, which was called an oval fruit bowl. It was deep cut and of sparkling clear crystal.

Card Tray whimsey. About 6" across with the four sides turned up to make it appear square in shape. This could be the same mould as the Applesauce Boat, since it's clear sparkling crystal with frosted feathers.

Compote. The same mould was used for the footed rose bowl. This is 5 1/4" tall, and the diameter of the bowl is 6". It was a welcome addition to my collection.

Cracker jar. Reported to me, and it must be quite rare, although it was advertised in 1910 Butler Brothers catalogs.

Giant rose bowl. The glass is quite heavy, but very clear. It was made from the same mould as the iridescent one, and in crystal it is just as beautiful. It's 9" tall, and the bowl measures 7 1/2" in diameter. A giant whimsey similar to this is also reported.

Handgrip plate. This 7 1/2" diamond-shaped handgrip plate is the only one I've seen. It was sold at an auction in 1982.

Handled basket. This extremely rare piece, which measures 5" d., sold at auction for $175 in 1983.

Ice cream set. Reported to me. Although I have not seen the large bowl, I do have a small one, about 5" in diameter and very shallow.

Plate. Reported to me, but I am not certain of the size.

Punch set. This ranks as one of my top favorites in crystal. It has the deep cut appearance and is beautiful clear crystal. Space is needed to display this one.

Relish dish. This could also be a pickle dish, and it's known in many sizes.

Small rose bowl, stemmed. This piece stands 6" tall, and the bowl is pulled in beautifully; diameter at edge varies from 2" to 4". The stemmed base diameter is 4". Quite a desirable piece, and one with a pulled-in top sold for $200 in 1990.

Spittoon whimsey. Reported.

Stemmed sherbet. This stands 4" tall with a 3 7/8" diameter bowl.

Table set. This four-piece set—covered butterdish, covered sugar bowl, creamer and spooner—was reported to me, and I have seen some items, but not a butterdish. William Heacock showed a ruby-stained spooner in his *Collecting Glass*, vol. 2.

Tankard water set. This tankard measures 9 1/4" tall and its base shows a pontil mark. The tumbler is 4" tall, an unusual shape and beautiful. The glass is heavy and sparkling clear. Both examples are rare.

Honeycomb and Hobstar

This is a beautiful, well-designed vase with the clear brilliance of Millersburg crystal. I have seen only one, and no more have been reported. Very rare.

Marilyn

Seldom offered in crystal, this pitcher is worth waiting for, but I have never seen a tumbler. The imitation cut design is pretty, and the glass is clear and heavy. Why don't we see more of this pattern?

Ohio Star

This was the factory's pattern No. 353 and it was probably the first pattern made in May, 1909. Mould drawings for some pieces are dated April, 1909.

Several No. 353 Ohio Star punch bowls are visible between the people seated on this wagon. The specific occasion is not known for certain, but the patriotic decorations suggest a Fourth of July parade.

With this pattern, it's not difficult to summarize my description, and it will do for all examples I have seen in this beautiful design. The glass is thick and sparkling, and the shapes are well-designed. Whether showing examples alone or as a collection, it is spectacular.

Some examples have been reported to me, but I have not seen them: banana bowl; cookie jar; cruet; sherbet; square bowl with matching flat sauce dishes; tray whimsey; water bottle; and wine glasses. The known articles are listed below.

Berry bowl. The round master bowl is rather deep (about 3 1/2") and is 9" in diameter. Small ones, probably sauce dishes, are also found. The glass is thick but sparkling clear.

Cider set and *water set*. Either of these would be nice additions to a collection. The cider set features a tall, tankard style pitcher. I have been fortunate enough to find a tumbler.

Compotes. These are found in two sizes. One that is 7" tall, but looks taller at first, has a heavy, solid glass stem, but the bowl is shallow; this is extremely rare in crystal as well as Carnival glass. The other compote measures 4 3/4" tall, with bowl diameter of 5 1/4."

Punch set. I have only seen one complete 14-piece set. So huge and beautiful, this one is not easy to forget. Rare and not offered often.

Rose bowl, stemmed. Made from the same mould as the small compote, but with the top edge of the bowl pulled in. It measures 5" tall, and the pulled-in top is 3 1/2" in diameter. The base of the stem measures 4" and has a star bottom. This piece certainly rates as the star in any collection.

Rose bowl. Larger than usual, this one measures 7" across. Heavy clear crystal. These aren't easy to find, but I've seen one.

Salt/pepper shakers. These are known in two sizes. One is short and squat, while the other is taller. Extremely rare. One set sold in 1990.

Table set. This complete set has butterdish, creamer, sugar and spooner. These are almost impossible to find without some damage but all together the set is spectacular. We seem to forget this crystal was used by families. Clear, sparkling brilliance is still beautiful on the crystal.

Toothpick holder. This is another desirable example of Ohio Star, not only for the beauty but also as an historic piece of glass. Reportedly, these were given away when the factory first went into production.

Vase. Rarely found in this beautiful imitation cut design, this is about 10" tall. The glass is heavy and usually very clear and brilliant.

Editor's note: just before this book went to press, two Ohio Star compotes turned up in blue glass (not iridized)!

Palm Wreath

This pattern is "questionable" as being made by Millersburg. After comparing the hobstar design with Ohio Star, I would believe Millersburg until proven otherwise. The glass is heavy and has the clear brilliance of Millersburg. A bowl and a goblet have been reported.

Creamer. This could be part of breakfast set. It is an unusual shape; instead of being round, it is oblong with the hobstar directly under the spout and has a palm leaf design on the flat sides, which display the design very nicely. In clear sparkling crystal, it's very pretty.

Cruet. The cruet is 5 1/4" tall without the stopper and with a beautiful well-designed stopper it's 7 1/2" tall. A hobstar with a center similar to Ohio Star appears on each side, and two palm leaf designs complete the pattern.

Peacock and Urn

Only the large compote, with no pattern on the inside, has been reported.

Potpourri

This is an interesting imitation cut design with a daisy-like star design. There is also a hobstar design and fan separated by arches. Potpourri always appears as an exterior or back pattern.

Compote. Potpourri is the exterior pattern found on iridescent Poppy compotes. One of the three shapes known is a compote that is 7" tall and 7" across the bowl, which has straight sides. This was described as "brilliant star and jewel panel design" and called a fruit bowl in a 1910 Butler Brothers catalog.

Bowl. This Popourri large round advertising piece bears these this message: "Louis Mankowitz Chicago."

Milk pitcher. Very pretty in crystal and quite rare.

Salver (footed). This rare piece is a flattened compote that is 7" tall and 8" across. It could be called a cake salver or a stemmed cake plate.

Trefoil Fine Cut

This is the exterior pattern on one reported bowl which is otherwise plain. It is also the back pattern on the Many Stars Carnival glass bowl.

Wild Flower

Known also as Millersburg Wild Flower, this is a scarce pattern. Only the compote has been reported.

Wild Rose Lamp

This is not Millersburg, but it probably was produced from an original Millersburg mould which was altered. It is marked "Riverside."

In addition to the patterns listed above, there are probably other Millersburg crystal patterns that aren't yet reported. Any examples found of the patterns listed do make an interesting, beautiful collection. Finding other patterns would add to this. One wonders when the Mayflower and Near-Cut Wreath bowls (shown in 1910-1912 Butler Brothers catalogs) will turn up.

Editor's note: The court-ordered inventory (dated April 10, 1911) of the Millersburg glass plant provides an interesting picture of the crystal glassware then in stock. Many items in the No. 400 (a colonial-style pattern) are listed, and there are quite a few pieces in both No. 353 Ohio Star and No. 358 Hobstar and Feather. The factory had quantities of some articles in stock, such as the "No. 105 7" berry Radium" (173 dozen) and the "No. 400 basket" (166 dozen). The patterns are typically identified only by number (e. g., No. 110, No. 400, No. 410, and No. 500), and there are many individual items which were not part of a pattern line: No. 40 sweet pea vase, No. 103 berry, No. 107 7" nappy, No. 217 tumbler, and No. 485 jardinere. One of the more mysterious items is the "No. 110 Chop Suey."

MILLERSBURG CRYSTAL AUCTION PRICES

At an auction in1982, these prices were realized: Hobstar and Feather pattern: stemmed rose bowl, $105; relish dishes. $75-80; spade-shaped sauce, $55; (3) 5" round sauce dishes, $17.50 each; handgrip plate, 7 1/2" diamond-shaped, $60; oval fruit bowl, $80; stemmed sherbet, $25; water set, six-piece with tankard pitcher, $325; giant rose bowl, $425; ten-piece banquet punch set, $1,275. Feather and Heart pitcher, $95. Marilyn pitcher, $155. Potpourri pattern: large square bowl, $65; large flat plate, $80; compote, $100; large round advertising bowl, "Louis Mankowitz, Chicago," $80; milk pitcher, $190. Ohio Star pattern: toothpick, damaged, $65; large rose bowl, $175; tankard pitcher, $325; four-piece table set (two nicks on sugar lid), $200; vase, $115; 14-piece punch set, $650; compote (very rare), $300.

At an auction in 1983, these prices were realized for pieces in Millersburg's Hobstar & Feather: punch bowl and base ($550); stemmed sherbet ($15); 8" bowl, frosted ($55); stemmed compote ($25); handled basket 5" ($175); and ice cream bowl ($100). A Potpourri compote brought $35, and an Ohio Star Vase $70. The Wild Rose kerosene lamp from the Riverside mould brought $75.

At an auction in 1990, these prices were realized: Ohio Star pattern: salt/pepper shakers (extremely rare), $80; four-piece table set, $195; compote, tall, $75; round bowl, $45. Hobstar and Feather small stemmed rose bowl, $200. Country Kitchen 9" plate with Bijou Theatre ad, $75. Country Kitchen 8" bowl with Illinois Furniture Co. advertising, $65.

CHAPTER TWO

Millersburg's Carnival Glass

There are so many variations and sizes from the same pattern moulds, that it's easy to become confused. In this chapter, each pattern known to have been made by Millersburg in Carnival glass will be discussed, including shapes, colors and sizes. I have seen many of the examples noted here, but some were reported to me by fellow collectors.

Millersburg didn't make as many colors as some of the other glass companies which produced Carnival glass. They stayed with basic colors, sometimes with a slightly lighter or darker shade, but not enough to warrant defined divisions like the pastels of Northwood or Dugan. In either natural or artificial light, iridescent glass shows many rainbow colors. The base color of any example is the true color of the glass before it was iridized. Ruby or red base glass was not made by Millersburg.

Amethyst was used as a base color by Millersburg more than any other, and it is seen in several shades. The term "amethyst" is typically used more to describe the color, but some examples are nearly a dark purple. Another rarely seen shade is lavender.

Green is one of the outstanding Millersburg colors, especially when the radium finish is displayed. Olive green, aqua and teal are known but rarely seen.

Millersburg's marigold Carnival ranges from a pale pastel to a deep, dark color. Some patterns are extremely rare in marigold. The shades rarely seen are called honey amber and clambroth by some collectors. Editor's note: The court-ordered inventories of the Millersburg plant in 1911 list only two Carnival glass hues. The term "Radium" is used often and was probably applied in a general way to virtually all the iridescent glass colors. The other term, "Golden," appears just once ("358 Punch Bowls Golden"), and it refers to marigold punch bowls in the No. 358 (Hobstar and Feather) pattern.

Millersburg iridescent ware in Butler Brothers catalogs, 1911.

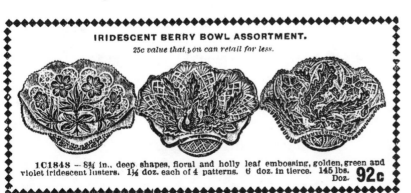

Blue is very rare and not found in all patterns. Some examples are known with very dark blue, while others are not the best color or good iridescence usually expected of Millersburg. But, with blue being rare and highly desirable, the selling price remains high regardless of the color. It just has to be blue!

Vaseline has a yellow base color with a greenish tint. Some examples have better iridescence and a deeper greenish tint. Natural light shows vaseline at its best. If in doubt, put the example under a black light (i. e., ultrviolet light) and any vaseline will fluoresce. Black light is rarely needed to identify Millersburg's vaseline.

White Carnival glass is usually described as a crystal clear base glass with frosty white iridescence. A strong frosty tint is the most desirable. An Ohio Star Vase is known is this color.

Few assortments of Millersburg's iridescent glass have been found in Butler Bothers catalogs. Collecting, taking notes, attending conventions and auctions, photographing Carnival glass and the generous help of many collectors has made the above information possible.

As Millersburg Carnival glass continues toward the top as a collectible item, additional facts will come to light. More and more of the rare colors become known. The comments below are from what I have learned and as I know the glass. If you find omissions or mistakes, please let me hear from you. It takes teamwork and sharing knowledge to maintain this interesting hobby.

Acorn

The stemmed compote with cloverleaf style base is the only known piece in this pattern. It is a little under 6" tall with a ruffled or jelly type bowl. Very rare with known Carnival colors amethyst, green, two vaseline examples and one other reported. Only one marigold example known. An amethyst jelly type compote sold in 1982, and a green one in 1990. One vaseline example has changed owners several times. This beautiful compote is highly desirable and has an increasing market value.

Bernheimer Brothers

This 10" crimped, ruffled bowl is from the same mould as the Many Stars, but the center of the interior has a small five-pointed star and the lettering "BERNHEIMER BROTHERS." in a beaded circle. The back pattern is Trefoil Fine Cut. The only known Carnival color is blue. For both the true deep color and fine iridescence, this is one of the best of Millersburg's blues. It's not as rare as some other examples, but the high desirability keeps the market value strong.

Big Fish

Found in bowls only, this motif is more difficult to find than the Trout and Fly bowls. Among the differences are the flower designs with pretty water lilies added, the slightly smaller fish, and the absence of the fly. The design is quite realistic. Examples can be found in round, square and tri-cornered bowls with several edge variations. Carnival colors are amethyst, green, marigold and vaseline. Any Big Fish pattern in any color is a treasure in a collection. My favorites are the radium finish examples.

This ad appeared in the February 9, 1910, issue of *Pottery, Glass and Brass Salesman.*

A S AN EXHIBITION of alternating and intermingling colors, the grandest rainbow ever seen in eastern sky has nothing on

RADIUM GLASS

A different iridescent effect is produced on every individual piece.

RADIUM is an Art Glass for the masses—if you cater to them get in touch with us. RADIUM will double your sales. Hundreds of articles for every practical purpose you expect to find in glass.

THE MILLERSBURG GLASS CO.

MILLERSBURG, OHIO

Big Thistle

The punch set, known only in amethyst Carnival, is one of Millersburg's most desired rarities. Only two punch bowls and bases are known. No cups have been reported. One punch bowl has straight sides and the other one is flared out at the top. Of the four patterns for punch sets made by Millersburg, this is the only one that has the plain Wide Panel exterior pattern. I'm happy to show a picture of this punch bowl. You have to see this example to really appreciate the superior workmanship, deep color and iridescence. One of the added benefits of attending auctions and conventions is to see Carnival glass in person. Rarely ever offered for sale, this punch bowl was added to one collection in 1992 at the auction of the estate of Robert and Kitty Vining.

Blackberry Wreath

A later chapter on confusing patterns covers information and description of this pattern, but the basics regarding size, shape and color will be given here.

The 6" d. sauce dish comes in amethyst, green, and marigold Carnival in various shapes and with different edges. Recently, the small sauce dishes have become very popular, and this has increased prices. Many of the small examples have outstanding color and iridescence. More satin than radium finish examples are known. The 7" size is rarer, with one example in blue Carnival reported. Bowls 8" to 10" in diameter are known in amethyst, blue, green, and marigold Carnival. The shapes include round, tri-cornered, and the large ice cream. The edges are six-ruffled, candy ribbon edge tightly crimped, and the three-in-one edge.

The ice cream bowls are highly desirable in all colors, especially the blue. Flat plates (6" d.) are rare, with half a dozen or so known in both amethyst and marigold Carnival. The green 8" flat plate has only one known, and it's a super example. The large chop plate finds just two amethyst and one marigold Carnival reported.

Only one 7" rose bowl is known in marigold Carnival, but three examples of the spittoon whimsey are known in marigold Carnival.

Boutonierre Compote

This compote is approximately 5" tall with a bowl 5" diameter on a stemmed base (3" d.). The interior of the bowl has a single flower with five petals. There are variations of bowl shapes; some are ruffled, but others are pulled in tight and some are flattened with the edges turned up. Colors are amethyst, green, and marigold Carnival. All have outstanding color and super iridescence in either radium or satin. Amethyst is most desirable and has the highest market value, but green and marigold Carnival are more difficult to find. For a less expensive item, these are good choices. Wouldn't a blue or vaseline compote be a real find?

Bull's Eye and Loop Vase

This is one of the patterns that was generally unknown to early collectors. The examples I have seen have good color and the radium finish. There is a variety of sizes from the shortest, 7" tall, through those 8" and 9" up to an 11" example. I've seen amethyst and green Carnival, but purple and a marigold/vaseline example have been reported, too.

Campbell and Beesley Co.

This advertising item says "Campbell & Beesley Co. Spring Opening 1911." Only a handgrip plate is known, and it's amethyst Carnival. The back pattern is Wide Panel. This is a very plain design with leaves and single flowers, and the advertisement on an unserrated edge example makes it equal to the Court House bowl. This item is quite scarce, with only fewer than a dozen examples offered at auctions in the past ten years. With the strong demand for advertising examples among many collectors, it's difficult to add this handgrip plate to a Millersburg collection. The unique shape, design, color and iridescence make it worth the wait.

Cherry, Millersburg

See Hanging Cherries, the name most collectors use now.

Cleveland Memorial

This souvenir ash tray measures 6" diagonally and is rare. Some examples are damaged, but the high desirability and rarity keep prices high. A fine example of one of these sold for $8,000 in June, 1994. Colors are amethyst and marigold Carnival.

See the very interesting article on this and other advertising examples in John Resnik's *Encyclopedia of Carnival Glass Lettered Pieces.* [editor's note: Resnik believes that this piece was sold at the Cleveland Industrial Exposition in June, 1909. If this is correct, the Millersburg plant must have been making iridescent ware at its inception in May, 1909. Trade journal reports are not conclusive, but they suggest that Millersburg's Radium ware was not perfected until early in 1910. Marigold Hobstar and Feather items were in Butler Brothers catalogs by December, 1909, however].

Cosmos

Just three pieces can be found, all in green Carnival: the 6" ice cream shape, a 6" plate, and a deep ruffled sauce dish. These have a nice green Carnival color with excellent iridescence, and they aren't particularly hard to find. The value varies little, but they are nice additions to a collection.

Country Kitchen

With so many articles from this pattern line found in crystal, it's a mystery why so few were made in Carnival glass. Perhaps the manufacturers were simply more interested in other motifs when making iridescent ware.

Large berry bowls large are known in several shapes along with some small bowls. The only color I've seen is marigold Carnival, and these are seldom offered for sale.

The four-piece table set (butterdish, covered sugar bowl, spooner and creamer) is very rare, but complete sets are known in both amethyst and marigold Carnival. The covered sugar bowl and the spooner are reported in vaseline Carnival.

A Country Kitchen spittoon whimsey is one of the top rarities in Millersburg Carnival, with only one known in amethyst Carnival. This piece began with the spooner mould and was shaped into a whimsey.

Swung vases, also classified as whimseys, were also made from the spooner mould. These are very rare in amethyst or marigold Carnival.

Court House

This bowl is known in the 7" size only. This design, of course, was based on the Holmes County court house located in Millersburg. The quality of the design, along with fine color and iridescence, make it one of the most popular examples and desired by all collectors.

Amethyst Carnival is the only color known, with the ice cream shape displaying the design at its very best. These are found in either radium or satin finish. Bowls are also found in the six-ruffled shape, and an extremely rare three-in-one edge is also known. All have the Wide Panel back pattern.

The bowl is usually lettered as follows: MILLERSBURG SOUVENIR COURT HOUSE MILLERSBURG OHIO. The "unlettered" bowls say simply MILLERSBURG SOUVENIR.

According to local legend around Millersburg, this souvenir bowl was one of the many gifts from John W. Fenton. As the story goes, these bowls were given as a tribute to the people who helped with the gas lines to the factory.

Deep Grape

The compote is the usual piece in this pattern. It stands 7" tall with a top opening from 5" to 7" in either round or square shape. One amethyst Carnival compote has the candy ribbon edge. The typical colors known are amethyst, green, or marigold Carnival, and one compote is reported in blue Carnival.

The only known Deep Grape rose bowl (in green Carnival) is 7 1/8" high with a 3 3/4" top opening. This is a beautiful piece and a top rarity. This rose bowl sold in 1991 for $7,000.

Diamonds

The punch bowl and base are very rare, with single examples known in amethyst, green and marigold Carnival. A few amethyst

bases exist, and one green bowl has been reported. Curiously, no cups are known in any Carnival color. The base to the punch bowl can be inverted and used by itself as a nice compote.

Water sets are known in amethyst, green, and marigold Carnival with aqua reported. This pattern is the easiest to find of all Millersburg water sets. An odd pitcher, made without the pouring spout, is known in both amethyst and green Carnival.

The spittoon whimsey is certainly rare, as just one marigold example is known. It sold at the Britt auction in March, 1994, for $7,000.

Dolphins Compote

Again we see John W. Fenton's creative ability in an entirely different design for a compote. It has outstanding workmanship. The bowl is larger in diameter than most compotes, supported by three dolphins attached to the base [editor's note: one of the court-ordered inventories of the Millersburg plant's glassware lists the "410 Dolphin Comport"].

This piece has the Rosalind interior pattern. Some are damaged, but due to the scarcity and desirability, it doesn't seem to lower the value very much. Colors are amethyst, blue and green Carnival. This is one of the prettiest compotes. Wouldn't it be exciting to find a marigold example?

Elk

Amethyst Carnival is the only color known in the 7" bowl with the Wide Panel back and excellent radium finish. The Millersburg Elk is "two-eyed" and the lettering says "Detroit 1910, B.P.O.E." [Benevolent and Protective Order of Elks]. The ice cream shape displays the superb artistry of this design to better advantage than the ruffled bowls. Not easy to find in either shape, these are popular with all collectors.

Elk paperweight

This is a heavy piece of glass which measures 4" x 2 2/3" x 7/8" thick. It has a flat surface displaying the Elk's head, with the clock above and the B.P.O.E. emblem. Apparently, these paperweights were well used, since many are damaged. Quite a few amethyst Carnival examples are known, but most have moderate damage. Of two known green Carnival examples, one is damaged.

Feather and Heart

Water sets are the only known articles in this imitation cut design in heavy glass. The pitcher is 7" tall, and the amethyst and marigold Carnival are offered more often than the green or vaseline Carnival examples. Some lack good color, but complete water sets are scarce. This is a pretty design. A vaseline Feather and Heart pitcher brought $14,000 in October, 1994, and a spittoon-like whimsey made from a tumbler was also sold.

Fleur De Lis

This is an outstanding design using a motif associated with the royal families of France. Three leaves of petals resembling an iris or lily with a bar near the base encircle the interior of the bowls. The back pattern is Country Kitchen. With the radium finish, the two patterns combine together in a beautiful example for any collection. Fleur De Lis is also an interior pattern on some Hobstar and Feather punch bowls.

A wide choice of bowls in many sizes and shapes can be found in either satin or radium finish. Bowls with the collar base are harder to find than the domed base. Amethyst, green, and marigold Carnival are best known, and one vaseline Carnival bowl has come to light. Bowls with the domed base are known in a deep round bowl with three-in-one edge as well as the ice cream shape and a tri-cornered bowl. Tri-cornered examples have brilliant radium iridescence and good color; these are highly desirable.

With only one compote now known (in green Carnival), I believe this is a previously unlisted example. It was in California for a short time, but it soon found its place in a Millersburg glass collection in Illinois. Two different rose bowls (collar base or domed base) exist, but there are only two examples of each in amethyst Carnival. The compote and these rose bowls are top Millersburg rarities.

Flowering Vine

This compote measures 9" tall, with the bowl opening 6 3/4" in diameter. Only one example is known in green Carnival, but there are two in amethyst Carnival. The green Carnival compote sold in 1982 for $1,300, and in 1990 it brought $3,750. It was sold again in 1994 (back to its previous owner) for $9,500. One amethyst Carnival compote has been in a California collection for many years. Neither of the known amethyst Carnival examples have been offered for sale. This is certainly one of the most beautiful of the Millersburg compotes.

Flute

With all the Flute patterns made in Carnival glass at various factories, there has been controversy about this one. Some collectors do not believe it was made by Millersburg, while others firmly believe it was. Editor's note: fragments found at the factory site leave no doubt that Millersburg made a colonial style pattern designated No. 400. It is variously known as Flute, Wide Panel or "unpatterned" among Carnival glass collectors today.

The clarity of the amethyst base color is good, and the examples I have seen have the very good iridescence typical of Millersburg. It has the same flutes and cloverleaf base used by Millersburg on the Wild Flower compote.

The Flute pattern occurs in punch sets, in berry sets with small round sauce dishes, and also vases which have excellent color and iridescence. Amethyst Carnival is the color usually seen, except for the reports of several blue Carnival vases.

Edwards renamed the small sauce dish that he showed in *Millersburg, Queen of Carnival Glass*. His new name is Flute and Honeycomb, instead of Variant. Discon-tinuing any variant name makes patterns much easier to identify. More information on this rare compote can be found in the section on unpatterned compotes.

Fruit Basket

The two-handled footed bon-bon is the only article here, and the only known color is amethyst Carnival. The interior has a basketweave design with various fruits (pineapple, grapes, pear, apple and cherries) in the center along with beautiful stippled leaves. Due to the intricate design, the Fruit Basket was probably difficult to produce. The moulds were modified to make the Roses and Fruit bon-bon, since both are from the same mould and have the same exterior pattern. With only four or five examples known, the Fruit Basket is rarely offered for sale and has always had a high market value.

Gay Nineties

Pieces are extremely rare, especially the water pitcher with only one green and three amethyst Carnival known. This pattern has always rated near the top of the Carnival glass water sets. There are quite a few amethyst Carnival tumblers reported, but just two marigold Carnival examples are known.

Grape Leaves

This pattern is found only in bowls, and the Carnival colors range from amethyst, green and marigold to one bowl known in vaseline Carnival. There are excellent examples in every shape, and they usually come with super color and iridescence. The pattern not easily found, but it's worth the wait. See the chapter on "Confusing Patterns."

Grape Wreath and Grape Wreath Variant

For complete details, read the section devoted to these motifs under "Confusing Patterns."

Greengard Furniture Co.

Another very rare lettered example with only one ruffled bowl and three double hand-grip plates in amethyst Carnival reported, these are among Millersbirg's best as to deep, dark color coupled with neat design and excellent iridescence. The lettering reads as follows: "Greengard Furniture Co., 11020 Mich. Ave, Roseland Ill."

Original mould drawing for Millersburg's Hanging Cherries; the sketch bears the words "Jug Cherries design." *Courtesy of the Fenton Museum.*

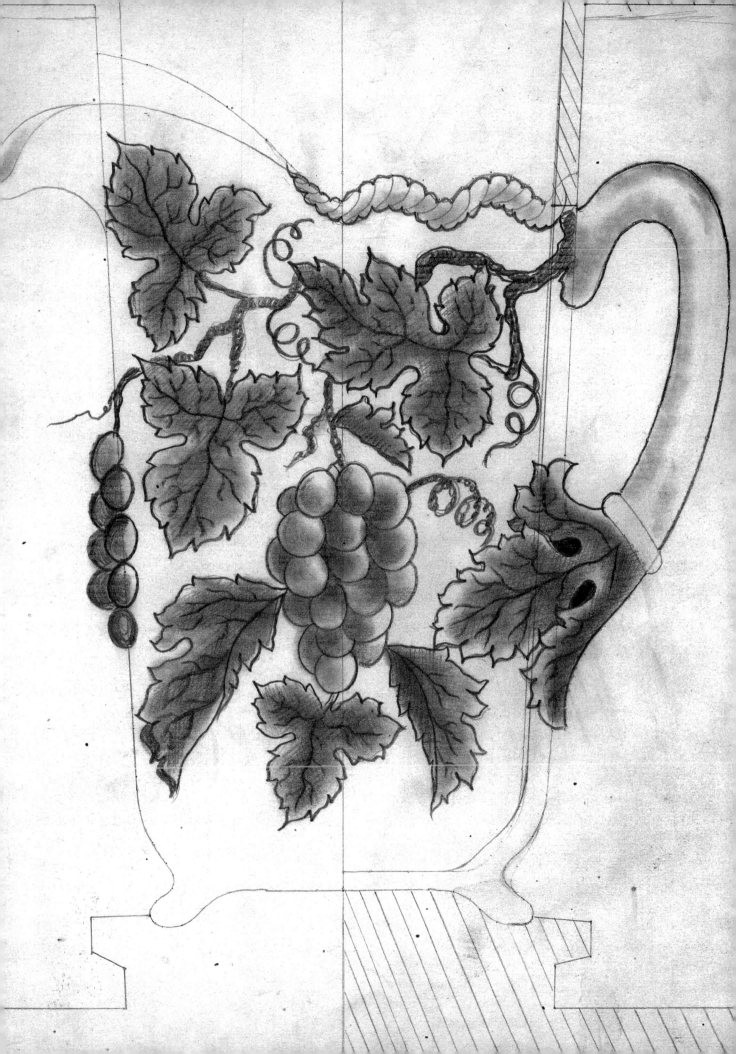

Hanging Cherries

With a definite design of hanging cherries and stippled leaves, this name makes it easier to identify, although it was called Millersburg Cherries for many years. Examples are found in either satin or radium finish. Since it was probably one of the early patterns in iridescent ware, we see more satin than radium examples.

Sauce dishes, 4" to 5" d., can be found, including the ice cream shape, the three-in-one edge and the ruffled edge. Colors include amethyst, blue, green, and marigold Carnival.

The 7" very shallow round bowl has been called a plate, but it isn't flat enough; for me it's a bowl (even if I did pay the price of a plate!). Super color and iridescence are found on these examples. The same size is known in a six-ruffled bowl, but it is rarely seen. Plain backs are rarely seen on Millersburg, but I have seen a 10" Hanging Cherries bowl with the plain back and a three-in-one edge.

Rather deep bowls, 9" d. in a round shape are known as are 5" sauce dishes to make a berry set. Complete sets are rare, although marigold Carnival is known, and a green Carnival set was reported. I have never seen a set in amethyst. Fluted 9" bowls are reported in amethyst, green and marigold Carnival. The 10" bowls are usually seen in ruffled or ice cream shapes. Colors are amethyst, blue, green and marigold Carnival. Radium finish large ice cream bowls are difficult to find in any color. The large bowl is also known in aqua Carnival.

Bowls with the Hobnail exterior are known in the 10" size. they are rare, and eight to ten examples are known in amethyst Carnival. Marigold Carnival is harder to find; I have only seen four examples. Two blue Carnival bowls are known, and one in green Carnival is reported. One 5" sauce dish exists in blue Carnival, too.

The large compote is 6" tall, with the bowl opening 7" in diameter and an unusual, beautifully-designed stem with a 4" diameter base. These are rare, and very few are ever offered for sale. The color is very good, and these have excellent iridescence; my favorite is the amethyst Carnival. Only one example in blue Carnival is known. Marigold and green Carnival examples exist, with green the harder to find. There is also a large compote whimsey, with the top shaped like the banana boat, in amethyst Carnival. I have not seen this unusual compote, but it's pictured in Edwards' *Millersburg, The Queen of Carnival Glass.* (p. 113)

The Hanging Cherries milk pitcher is much rarer than the water pitcher. Colors available are amethyst, green, and marigold Carnival, with amethyst being hardest to find.

Several sizes of plates exist in various colors as indicated here: 6" plate, marigold Carnival only; 8" flat plate, amethyst and green Carnival known; 9" plate, amethyst Carnival reported; 10" chop plate, green and marigold Carnival known; amethyst reported.

The four-piece table set is probably the easiest of all Millersburg table sets to find in amethyst, green or marigold Carnival. In blue Carnival only a few pieces are known. I have seen two butterdishes with aqua bases and green lids.

The Hanging Cherries powder jar is an outstanding Millersburg rarity, and just one is known (in green Carnival).

The water pitcher, while rare, is known in amethyst, green and marigold Carnival, with the latter hardest to find. There are two slightly different tumblers: one tumbler has flared sides and is 4" tall, 3" d. with a base diameter of 2". Its bottom is not ground. This example is harder to find than the tumbler with straight sides which is listed as Variant in Owen's book on tumblers. This also measures 4" tall, but the top is 2 3/4" in diameter and the ground base measures 2 1/8" in diameter; the base has the many-rayed star. Both kinds of tumblers come in amethyst, green and marigold Carnival.

[Editor's note. In the October 8, 1987, issue of the *Holmes County Farmer-Hub*, Lucille Lowe related this about John W. Fenton's interest in cherries: "It is said that the Millersburg glass maker had a special fondness for sweet Black heart cherries and there were several of these trees near the plant. At the noon hour he would entice some of the younger men to climb a tree and throw down small limbs to him. The famous Millersburg Hanging Cherries pieces are a special depiction he made of his favorite fruit."

Hobnail

This is a highly desirable pattern and is rare in any color. Usually blue Carnival is the rarest, but green Carnival is also very difficult to find. Complete table sets are very rare, so the sugar, creamer and spooner are usually listed separately. Colors are amethyst, blue, green and marigold Carnival. A table set reported in blue Carnival apparently has an amethyst Carnival butter base.

Pitchers are rarely offered for sale, although a few amethyst, blue, and marigold Carnival examples have been sold at auctions. In 1989, a green Carnival pitcher was sold. Private sales and trades seem to be popular among pitcher and tumbler collectors. Of all colors known in Hobnail pitchers and tumblers, green Carnival is the rarest.

Both the rose bowl and a spittoon come in amethyst, green and marigold Carnival, but green is the rarest. A green vase, made from the from the same mould, is also quite rare.

Hobnail Variant has also been accepted as a pattern made by Millersburg, but some collectors will have reservations. Among the shapes known are the jardiniere whimsey, the rose bowl, and vases. The colors reported are amethyst, green and marigold Carnival. The rose bowl is a nice addition to any collection. The vases are pretty, and some are reported in blue Carnival.

Hobstar and Feather

This is one of the most popular of the imitation cut designs from 1909 and was surely one of the first patterns made by Millersburg in iridescent glass. A Butler Brothers catalog from December, 1909, shows the punch set and says that it was available in either crystal or ""allover fired golden iridescent finish."

All examples are thick, heavy glass with deep colors and good iridescence. The range of Carnival colors suggests that this pattern could have been made from time to time during Millersburg's productive periods. Although there are quite a few different pieces, few of any particular article are seen, so they must be considered scarce.

Just one square bowl (8 3/4" x 3 3/4" deep) with excellent iridescence is known in amethyst Carnival. Several examples of the 6" ice cream shape sauce dish exist in amethyst Carnival. Two of the bridge set pieces—heart and diamond—are known in marigold Carnival glass. The small compote, 5" tall with a bowl 6" d., occurs in marigold Carnival, and it has a clear stemmed base.

MASSIVE "SUNFLOWER AND LEAF" DESIGN PUNCH SET.

It's equal in quality and design never priced as low.

1C1983—Diam. deeep bowl 15½ ht. with separate stand 13, brilliant extra heavy pressed crystal, finest fire polish, twin sunflower panels with prominent leaves, deep notched scallop edge; 12 full size handled cups. 1 set in pkg.   Per set, **$2.35**

1C1984—Allover fired golden iridescent finish, otherwise as 1C1983. 1 set in pkg.   Per set, **$2.95**

The two-piece punch bowl is known in two styles: the flared bowl has been found in amethyst, green and marigold Carnival, with green being hardest to find. There are three green bowls known, but all have bases that are not green. Some of these punch bowls are found with Fleur De Lis as an interior pattern; the others are plain inside. The bowl with a "tulip top" is very rare, and only amethyst Carnival has been seen.

The punch bowl base only is known in vaseline; two are known with two others reported. This can be rated as one of the best of vaseline examples. Where is the punch bowl? Just one punch cup, in blue Carnival, has come to light. It was sold at auction in 1991. Punch cups in amethyst, green and marigold can be found for a complete set.

The giant Hobstar and Feather rose bowl is a massive piece of glass that weighs six pounds!. It stands 9" tall and has a 7" cupped, flower-shaped bowl with a turned-in scalloped top; the bottom of stem base has a large hobstar. The Carnival glass colors include amethyst, green and, rarest of all, marigold; I have seen two in marigold Carnival.

The whimsey punch bowl is shaped from the giant rose bowl and is flared out at the top. Rarely offered for sale, a green one sold in 1991 for $4,750. The giant whimsey cuspidor is shaped from the rose bowl. It is cupped in and flared at the top. This cuspidor is shown on the cover of the third edition of Edwards' book. In purple, it sold for $5,000 in 1991.

A swung vase (sometimes called a "whimsey") occurs in both amethyst and green Carnival, and two are known in each of these colors. One with a crimped top has been reported in amethyst Carnival.

Items from the four-piece table are known in several different colors, but a complete set in any one color has yet to turn up. The butterdish, covered sugar bowl and spooner are known in amethyst Carnival, and a green Carnival creamer has been seen. Two spooners have been reported in vaseline Carnival along with a sugar lid. The spooner is also known in marigold Carnival. An electric green spooner sold at auction in October, 1994.

Holly Sprig or Holly Whirl

Several items in this pattern are easily found: the bon-bon, the bowl, and a card tray. The small compote, the deep sauce dish and the rose bowl whimsey are rare. The small compote is the same shape as the Strawberry Wreath compote, and only about five of these are known in amethyst and marigold. These compotes were first reported to me after I had listed compotes in a newsletter.

Some 10" Holly Sprig bowls with the Near Cut Wreath exterior pattern are known in the ruffled or the ice cream shapes. The ruffled has a variation in the Holly Wreath interior pattern; added leaves cover the center of the bowl. The ice cream shape does not have the added leaves. The bowl with the exterior pattern is hard to find. Bowls 6' to 10" diameter typically have the Wide Panel exterior. Square or tri-cornered bowls are rarely for sale. The 6" deep sauce dish is a rare, desirable example. The colors known are amethyst, green, and marigold Carnival with the rose bowl whimsey in vaseline Carnival only.

Holly Sprig variants are known but are rarely seen. These have a center design like the Grape Wreath variant. The Holly patterns are usually good radium finish, but satin is also seen in these 7" or 8" bowls. Edwards mentions a variant with multi-ringed stars; at one time, I had a green Carnival 8" bowl in this variation.

Honeycomb and Hobstar

How can I describe the beauty of this vase? It stands 8 1/4" tall and has a stemmed base. Two amethyst are known; one blue is known and another blue reported. In May, 1987, this vase was offered for the first time at auction, and it was sold for $6,500. Reportedly, it was from the Bennetts' museum in Cambridge, Ohio. Another "Star" for Millersburg!

Isaac Benesch

Of great interest is the Isaac Benesch advertising found on a bowl with Wide Panel back. Although some attribute this to the Fenton plant in Williamstown, the fragments found at Millersburg suggest otherwise. The typical color is amethyst, but marigold may also be available. At least one bowl is known with a misspelling, i. e., Benech instead of Benesch.

Leaf and Little Flowers

This miniature compote is 3" tall, and the bowl diameter is 3 3/4." These are found with round or ruffled tops in amethyst, green and marigold Carnival. Marigold is the hardest to find, but the green and the amethyst ruffled types with radium finish usually bring the highest prices. This is the same mould as the very rare Olympic compote, but it displays a different interior design.

Little Stars

For so long, only a few shapes and sizes were seen in this pattern, but recently there have been exciting finds. This pattern is one of the rising stars of Millersburg glass.

Bowls 7" to 8" d. are the ones usually seen. Shapes range from the ruffled, the three-in-one edge and, most difficult to find, the ice cream shape (these show the pattern well and have a higher market value). The 8" to 9" sizes in the ice cream shape are popular and scarce. One 9" green Carnival with radium finish and a tight crimped edge is known. Another is a candy ribbon edge in lavender Carnival; it's a pretty bowl.

Two 9" bowls are reported in green and marigold Carnival, and a 10" example is also reported in green Carnival. Of the three usual Millersburg Carnival colors, marigold is the hardest to find in this pattern, but it is usually a deep color with excellent iridescence. These are known in the rare 6" ice cream shape sauce dish: one amethyst, two blue and two green examples.

Recently, another 6" ruffled sauce dish was been found in Ohio, a very nice blue Carnival. This makes three blue Carnival examples. In another update, a 10" blue Carnival ice cream bowl sold at auction November, 1993.

Many Stars

Always a popular pattern, Many Stars comes in amethyst, blue, green, and marigold Carnival. Also, two bowls are known in vaseline Carnival. More about the rare blue and vaseline Carnival bowls can be found later in this book.

Among the examples in the 9" and 10" size bowls are the ice cream shape, the ruffled, the three-in-one edge, and a tight crimped square bowl. Bowls have a five- or six-pointed star in the center (fewer examples with five-point stars seem to exist).

A large chop plate (flat 10 1/2" d.) with the Trefoil Fine Cut exterior was found in Texas. What a pleasure it was to see this top rarity. It's a deep, dark marigold Carnival color with good, all-over iridescence. A flat 10" chop plate is also known with the Trefoil Fine Cut exterior pattern, but this one has no pattern on the front; it's also Marigold Carnival, and has excellent iridescence.

Marilyn

This is one of Millersburg's imitation cut pattern lines produced about 1909-10 in crystal, but it is known only in water pitchers and tumblers in Carnival glass. This pattern is rarely offered for sale. Colors are amethyst, green and marigold Carnival, but green has a generally higher market value. As pretty as the Marilyn pattern is, we hear very little about it.

Mayan

This is an excellent example in an 8" or 9" green Carnival (radium finish) ice cream shape shallow bowl which is only 2" deep. It has a beaded button center, surrounded by six plumes within a beaded circle outer border. It has the Wide Panel back pattern with a star base. It's a unique design. In an aqua or olive green Carnival, these bowls are extremely rare. Green Carnival was the only color known until recently. A beautiful ruffled bowl in marigold Carnival with radium finish was found and is now in a Millersburg collection. From the owner's description, it's on the way to becoming a top rarity.

Mitered Ovals

All Millersburg vases are hard to find, and, with the great variety of shapes and patterns, how can a decision be made about which is prettiest or most desirable? In any case, Mitered Ovals is near the top.

These are 10 " tall and have a bulbous body and a ruffled top. They are rare and beautiful. Some have damage. About eight amethyst Carnival vases are known, and perhaps there are ten known in green Carnival. Marigold Carnival is the rarest, but any of these colors would have an estimated market value of $4,500 to $6,750.

Morning Glory

Only pitchers and tumblers are known. The pitcher is approximately 11" tall, usually found with a radium finish of majestic royal quality. Colors are amethyst, green and marigold Carnival with green the rarest.

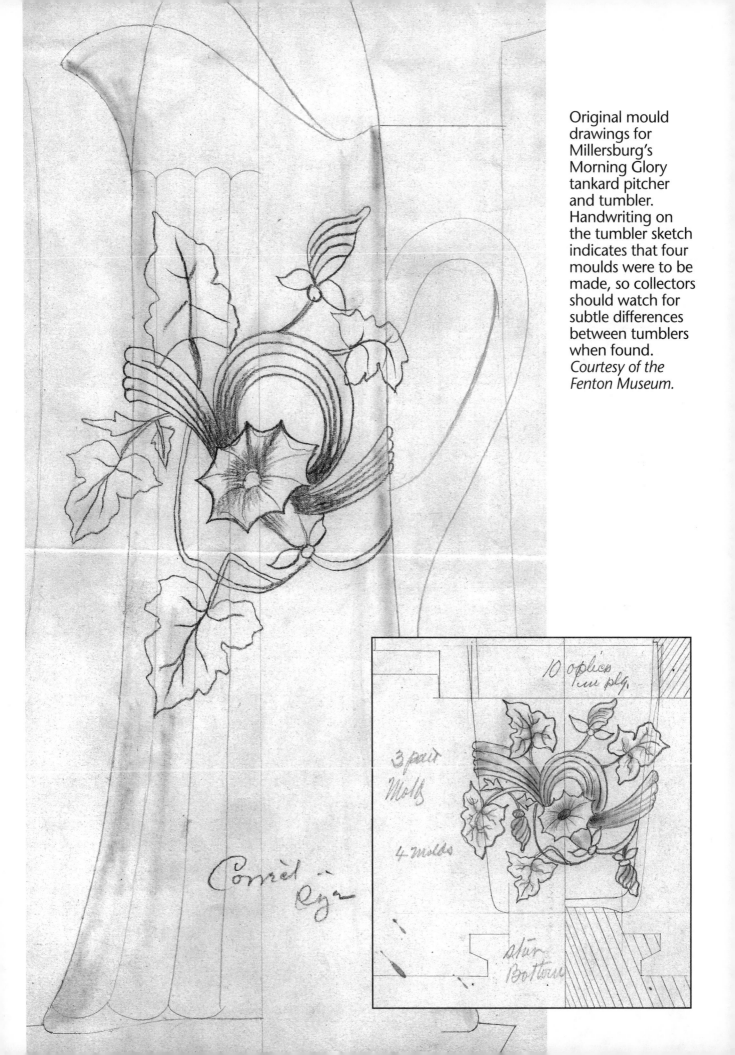

Original mould drawings for Millersburg's Morning Glory tankard pitcher and tumbler. Handwriting on the tumbler sketch indicates that four moulds were to be made, so collectors should watch for subtle differences between tumblers when found. *Courtesy of the Fenton Museum.*

Original mould
drawing for a
Multi-Fruits
and Flowers lid.
*Courtesy of the
Fenton Museum.*

This pattern has always rated among the rarest of all Millersburg water sets. Morning Glory is seldom offered for sale. The pitchers known and reported include four in amethyst, one in green, and three in marigold Carnival. Tumblers are also very rare. Fewer green and marigold are seen than amethyst Carnival. Because of the high desirability and rarity, the market value for Morning Glory pieces has always been very high.

Multi-Fruits and Flowers

This is another of Millersburg's fruit patterns, and it is one of the most popular. The only shapes known are pitchers, tumblers, punch sets and sherbet dishes. All are rare, usually with deep color and excellent iridescence. The base of the punch bowl doubles as a compote and can be beautifully displayed as a separate item.

Pitchers are extremely rare, and some are damaged. Among the known and reported are five in amethyst, one in green and two in marigold Carnival. One amethyst Carnival pitcher is known with painted fruit. Emma Tilton remembers owning this pitcher in the very early years of her collecting. It has surfaced once again, and I saw it on display at a convention. The rare tumblers are known in amethyst, green, and marigold Carnival.

Punch sets with flared tops are less difficult to find than tulip tops. Some I have seen have color and/or iridescence that is not very good. The Carnival colors found are amethyst, green, and marigold (green is hardest to locate). In punch sets with the tulip top, one each is known in amethyst, blue, and marigold, and two are known in green Carnival. Several blue Carnival bases minus bowls are known. A punch bowl was reported (May 1987, Lincoln Land newsletter) as having an inside bowl pattern. The pattern resembles a huge bunch of grapes and scroll-like filigree work. Named Scroll and Grape, this was reported later in Edwards' *Encyclopedia of Carnival Glass,* 3rd Rev. Ed. (p. 178) where a photograph is shown.

The Multi-Fruits and Flowers sherbet dish has been called a compote and sometimes a whimsey. It's very rare and desirable, and the colors known are amethyst and green Carnival. Several are damaged, but this doesn't alter the desirability or affect market values, which range from $200 to $850. Three green Carnival examples are known, and there are a few more in amethyst.

Nesting Swan

This design has the Diamond and Fan exterior pattern, and almost all Carnival glass collectors recognize the bowl and know that it was made by Millersburg. The typical colors are amethyst, green and marigold Carnival for these shapes: six-ruffled, 10" size, square, tri-cornered and the very popular candy ribbon edge bowls. Only one vaseline example and one blue bowl are known.

Seen most often is the 10" bowl that is ruffled or has a candy ribbon edge. The extremely rare 8" round bowl is another known example. An unusual color for Millersburg, collectors call it honey amber is also known. Green, square candy ribbon edge bowl is rare with two known, one other reported. Amethyst and marigold also reported. Tri-cornered examples with amethyst and green reported. Deep round bowl, one amethyst and one marigold known.

The rose bowl is rare, with just one reported in marigold Carnival. The spittoon whimsey is just about as scarce, with only one known in green Carnival.

[Editor's note. Lucille Lowe compiled this story of the inspiration for the Nesting Swan bowl (*Holmes County Farmer-Hub,* October 8, 1987):

"Another story was often told of the time Fenton, on the Millersburg train, brought two pairs of magnificent white swans home with him, forgetting no doubt, that swans need plenty of water. He however, devised large sunken troughs for his birds hoping this would content his large waterfowl. Suddenly the very first day, a cry of alarm went out from the plant employees as four big white birds took to the air flying right toward the Killbuck Creek. Fenton and his employees went running after them, but to no avail; the birds zoomed in on the old Killbuck and started paddling swiftly downstream while an excited John ran puffing along the creek bank. "The birds were never seen again. A couple of hours later, a very disappointed old glassmaker returned to his easel where he designed the beautiful Nesting Swan, even though the birds never even stayed long enough to build a nest."

Night Stars

A popular favorite is the Night Stars two-handled, oblong-shaped bon-bon. It has a star in the center, encircled with wreath-like design of six daisy flowers, and it is heavily stippled in center area. Colors known are amethyst, green, olive green (very rare), and marigold Carnival. Only four bon-bons are known in marigold Carnival. An amethyst Carnival tri-cornered nappy, the only one known, sold at auction for $900.

The card trays show this pattern at its best. All are extremely rare with one vaseline Carnival and one green Carnival known. One is also known in amethyst, but there could be more of these. Is there a marigold?

Ohio Star

This pattern has many different shapes in Millersburg's crystal glass, but only a few examples are known in Carnival glass .

The tall compote is known in marigold Carnival with a clear stem. A shorter, smaller compote is also known in marigold Carnival. Whimsey-type small relish dishes in marigold are also reported.

The most frequently seen examples are the beautiful vases. These stand 10" tall with an opening measuring 4" in diameter. They have a deep cut, star design pattern. In any of the Carnival colors—amethyst, green or marigold—the vases are rarely offered for sale. A mint condition premium example is almost impossible to find. More occur in green Carnival than the other colors.

Occasionally. vases are found in a swung vase shape. This is the normal shaped stretched out. These are much rarer than the other examples. An aqua opalescent vase is known, and there is a "frosty white" vase in a collection in Kansas. With the high desirability, the value remains high on any of these examples. Only four or five examples are known of the swung vase, including the aqua.

Olympic

This miniature compote measures 3" tall, and the bowl diameter is 3." It's from the same mould as the Leaf and Little Flowers. The center of bowl has a star with a circle of beads in a square, wreath-like design. It has eight smooth panels on the back and an octagon-shaped base. The only known amethyst Carnival example was sold at auction in 1990 for $2,850. The same compote was sold at the Britt's auction in 1994 for $4,600 to an Illinois collector. The only known green Carnival example sold in 1982. This is one of the top rarities in Millersburg glass.

Peacock patterns

What a choice of Peacock patterns we have by Millersburg! A large, super collection could be acquired by buying only Peacock patterns. There are bowls in all shapes and sizes, 6" plates, chop plates, rose bowls, and the giant compote. More questions have been asked about this motif than any other.

Based on my intensive study of these patterns since 1978, here are the rules I follow to identify each: the Millersburg Peacock has no bee and no beading on the Urn. Millersburg's Peacock and Urn may or may not have beading, but the bee is always there. Millersburg's Peacock and Urn "mystery" 8 3/4" bowl (earlier called a Variant) has two rows of beading and a larger bee. Millersburg's Peacock Variant "Shotgun" 7" size bowl has no beading and no urn, but it does have the bee. Millersburg's Peacock and Urn Variant 6" bowl (ice cream shape), has a bee and 3 rows of beading; with only about six examples known in amethyst Carnival, it is rare.

The chapter on "Confusing Patterns" will cover the sizes, shapes, colors and availability of the various Peacock patterns in detail.

[Editor's note. Lucille Lowe had this account of John W. Fenton's fondness for peacocks (*Holmes County Farmer-Hub*, October 8, 1987)]

"My grandfather always told of the love Fenton had for peacocks. The old glass maker surrounded himself and practically, the whole town of Millersburg, with the beautiful strutting birds. They flew hither and yon all over the village and lit any place their hearts desired. Seemed as though the court house steps, lawn and sidewalks were focal points.

"It was claimed that many taxpayers trying to enter the north door at the top of the steps had their minds changed and decided to use another door when they were met by a very angry old peacock with spread tail and wings, who claimed that area as his own. It is said that very few disputed the old bird unless they had a broom in hand. ... It is unknown as to where he derived the urn idea, perhaps from a piller high on those court house steps where his mighty old bird did reign, day in and day out from 1909-11. One day the vicious old bird never returned. Rumors were many as to the reason, but the Fenton already had depicted his pride and joy on glass and both his and our memories shall never vanish as long as we have our glass.

"Another story tells of how the mighty peacocks frightened the horses tied at the hitching rails located both on the east and west sides of the courthouse lawn. One day when a very skittish young team hauling a highpiled wagon load of ear corn was tied to the west rail, several of the screaming big birds lit all around them. In their fright, the team broke loose and at break neck speed, careened wagon and team right up East Jackson Street. As the wagon bounced so did the end gate, which became loosened and came completely off, to spray corn in all directions. Rumor had it that the team ran home near Berlin with nothing left but a wagon tongue and the neck yoke between them. This was one of my grandfathers favorite stories of those pesky peacocks owned by Fenton."

Peacock Tail Variant

This cute little compote is 3 1/4" tall, and the 6" d. bowl is on a very short stem with an octagon-shaped base that is 3" in diameter. The center of bowl has a feathered stippled rays effect and six-petal design. The known colors are amethyst, green and marigold Carnival with either a satin or a radium finish. This compote has excellent iridescence.

People's Vase

For many years, the People's vase has been rated as the top rarity of all Millersburg Carnival items. Many who aren't Millersburg collectors know of these vases and follow any news about them. There have probably been fewer changes of ownership among these vases than any other piece of Carnival glass. What a pleasure to be able to see three of these vases sitting side by side. Among the Carnival colors known are two amethyst, one blue, one green, and one marigold. All have straight sides except the two amethyst Carnival vases that have ruffled tops.

Editor's note: A court-ordered inventory (dated April 10, 1911) of the Milllersburg plant lists the No. 70 "Vase Holland" as an individual item not part of a pattern line. Only one dozen vases were then in stock, and, compared to other Millersburg glassware, they were rather expensive at $11.25 per dozen. The size and weight of the People's vase certainly qualify it as an expensive item, and the dancing characters depicted are not inconsistent with the term "Holland."

Perfection

The water pitcher in this pattern is not only very rare but also highly rated for beauty. The pitcher is 9" tall with a top opening 6" in diameter. It is the bulbous type and similar in shape to the Gay Nineties pitcher. One example in green Carnival has a ruffled top opening. In checking through auction records for the past 12 years, I found this pitcher is rarely offered for sale and felt happy to have an amethyst Carnival one in my collection. Only five other amethyst Carnival examples had been offered. A damaged green Carnival pitcher appeared several times, but further research showed it to be the same one offered over and over!

Amethyst Carnival is easier to find than green Carnival, and there are marigold Carnival pitchers reported. In the publications written by O. Joe Olson in 1978, almost all the Millersburg pitchers, especially Perfection, remained at the top in the opinion of most collectors.

Perfection tumblers are also very rare with only one green Carnival known and four marigold Carnival reported. Amethyst Carnival is much more readily found (see Figs. 187-188).

Pipe Humidor

This is one of the most popular Millersburg items and is desired by all collectors. The humidor is 8" tall and measures 5" across the top opening. The top of the bowl is encircled with acorns and leaves, and a leaf-like design extends up from the base.

The lid has a realistic smoker's pipe on top and a holder inside for a small sponge to keep the tobacco moist. All known examples have excellent color and iridescence. These are rarely offered for sale and will command a high price. With the help of Diane Fry, my research located six examples in amethyst, six in green, and eight in marigold Carnival.

Poppy

This compote is known in two shapes, both of which have an interior poppy design and the Potpourri design on the exterior. Seen most often is the 6" tall with a 7" d. deep bowl with slightly turned out edge. On the base of the stem, there's a small design of the Potpourri pattern. All of these compotes have good color and radium finish.

The flattened top compote is very rare. It stands 6" tall and the bowl is flattened (about 8" d.) with the edges of the bowl straight up. Known Carnival glass colors are as follows: one amethyst, two green, and one marigold. Of these three colors, marigold is more difficult to find in either of the two varieties.

Potpourri

This pattern is extremely rare, with only two marigold Carnival pitchers known. The interesting imitation cut design, coupled with super color and rarity, makes this a desirable item. These are rarely offered for sale, but one sold at an auction in 1990 for $1,600. Another sold in 1993 for $2,450.

Primrose

This pattern is often found in 10" bowls in amethyst, green and marigold Carnival with good color and iridescence. The Fine Cut Heart exterior pattern blends beautifully with the Primrose in either satin or radium finish. There is one vaseline Carnival bowl in a whimsey (banana boat) shape with a tightly crimped edge.

In the rare blue Carnival, three examples are known and another reported. It is interesting that the blue bowls are different shapes: six-ruffled, three-in-one edge, and ice cream shape. There is also an amethyst Carnival 8" bowl with excellent satin finish, but it is rarely seen. Any Primrose piece in any Carnival color makes a very nice addition to a collection.

Rays and Ribbons

This pattern doesn't get much attention except for the blue and vaseline Carnival bowls. With the exterior Cactus pattern combined with a stippled interior pattern, it's a pretty bowl.

There is a wide choice of shapes and edges. Carnival colors include amethyst, green, and marigold (as well as the two vaseline and two blue bowls known). An 8" round bowl, in heavy dark-colored glass that has to be purple, is known.

Another rarely seen Rays and Ribbons item is the 10" marigold Carnival bowl with an almost clear candy ribbon edge that turns out. One banana boat-shaped whimsey bowl is known in green Carnival, and a flat plate is reported in amethyst Carnival.

Rosalind

The 10" d. bowl is the size usually seen with the six-ruffled or a candy ribbon edge. The larger ice cream bowl is very rare, and examples measuring 8 1/4" to 9" are rarely seen. This size was flattened for the rare 9" plates. Any shape or size in this pattern is a nice addition to a collection.

An amethyst Carnival candy ribbon edge bowl with its super color and brilliant radium iridescence is rated among the superstars in my collection. Other Carnival colors known are green and marigold plus aqua teal, a very rare Millersburg color. The 6" sauce dish is also very rare. Examples known in the six-ruffled shape are two amethyst and four in green Carnival. The ice cream shape is known in green and marigold Carnival.

Rosalind compotes appear in two sizes. The extremely rare 6" version is known in amethyst and green Carnival. The large compote is 9" tall, with one example in amethyst being a jelly compote with a round bowl. The two marigold compotes are different. One has a round bowl 4" deep and 6" diameter, only slightly flared out at top. It has pastel marigold stem and a nine-panel base which is almost clear. The other compote has an open, ruffled bowl that shows the pattern very nicely. It has deeper color that extends to the stem and the base (one also known in blue).

In 9" plates, one amethyst is known, and 3-4 eamples in green have been reported.

Rosalind is also the interior pattern on the Dolphins compote.

Rose Column

Mould-blown vases only are the only articles known in this pattern. These stand 10" tall and are 5" in diameter across the top opening. Vertical rows of roses go from the base to a circle of leaves around the top. Some have damage from burst interior bubbles and others have some bad cracks, but all

"RADIUM" GLASS

Speaking of REAL Values in Iridescent Glass—Seen RADIUM?

Before placing your orders for Iridescent Glass this season, just look over the wonderful collection of values offered in RADIUM. We believe that in bulk, showiness and startling color effects, we have a perfect right to claim premier honors. Jobbers' Assortments, Five and Ten-Cent Specials. Our Sales Offices are now showing complete 1911 lines—drop in and look them over.

PAUL JOSEPH, 55 Park Place, New York, N. Y.   H. E. O'BRIEN, 12-14 State Street, Chicago, Ill.

GEO. REINHART, 617 Arch St., Philadelphia, Pa.   BARRIS & LINHARDT, 844 Pierce Bldg., St. Louis, Mo.

EDWIN F. BOKEE, 122 W. Baltimore St., Baltimore, Md.   ROBT. B. DUNN, Jr., 201 Columbia Bldg., Cleveland, O.

The Millersburg Glass Co.

This is the first advertisement in a glass trade publication which pictured Millersburg's wares; the next chapter of this book discusses the various centers found in Millersburg's Blackberry Wreath and Strawberry Wreath patterns.

"RADIUM" GLASS

We have purchased the plant and entire equipment of the Millersburg Glass Co., and are prepared to execute promptly, in ample time for

Holiday Trade

all orders for "RADIUM" GLASS specialties formerly made by the above concern. Jobbers' Assortments, Five, Ten and Twenty-five Cent Specials in the most beautiful iridescent colors ever produced.

The Radium Glass Co.

When the Radium Glass Company began making glass in the late fall of 1911, the firm used the same illustrations which had appeared in the Millersburg Glass Company advertisement months earlier.

are still desirable. Some amethyst and green Carnival ones are seen with poor color. As with all Millersburg vases, only a small number were made.

Today, it would be hard to estimate market value if a blue Carnival vase was offered or, for that matter, any color in mint condition. Colors usually seen are amethyst and green Carnival, as about a dozen are known in each of these colors. In marigold Carnival, about eight are reported to exist compared to just two in blue Carnival.. One blue Carnival vase sold for $8,000 in 1982. Also known is a single experimental amethyst Carnival vase with fired-on red, green and gold colors.

Roses and Fruit

This is a two-handled footed bon-bon from the same mould as the rare Fruit Basket. The bowl measures 5" between its handles and stands 4" tall. In the center of the bowl are a pear, grapes, berries and some stippled leaves. The upper inside edge has roses, rosebuds and leaves. The outside handles have stippled leaves also. Colors are amethyst, green, and marigold Canival; all are rare, with amethyst seen more often than green or marigold Carnival. One blue Carnival example is known, and another is reported.

Seacoast

The scarce Seacoast pin tray measures 5" long by 4" wide, and it has an oblong collar base. The design consists of a fish and a background coast line complete with a lighthouse and the rising sun.This is fantastic art work in such a small area. Known colors are amethyst, green and marigold Carnival with an excellent radium finish. The marigold is very difficult to find.

This piece is popular with all collectors, so the market value remains high. Editor's note: One of the court-ordered inventories of the Millersburg plant in 1911 lists "Fish and Sunflower Pin Trays." The company had 160 dozen on hand at the time, and the wholesale price was $1.00 per dozen.

Seaweed

Here again, Millersburg used the same pattern for a variety of shapes and sizes in the Seaweed bowls. Most commonly seen is the 10" bowl with ruffled or three-in-one edge. The 9" bowl in either the ruffled or the ice cream shape is much rarer. The 8 1/4" size is extremely rare, and it is the one flattened for the 9" plate. Large ice cream bowls are difficult to find, but they display this beautiful pattern to its best advantage. Known colors are amethyst, green and marigold Carnival. One large ice cream bowl in blue Carnival is also known, and another example is known in aqua teal, a very rare color for Millersburg.

Rarest of all are the 5" sauce dishes. In the ruffled sauce dishes, one each is known in amethyst, blue and marigold Carnival. One blue Carnival small ice cream shape is known, and one in green has been reported.

In plates, the 9" size is known in amethyst, green, and marigold Carnival. Sometimes this plate is questionable since Millersburg is known for its truly flat plates. Two very flat green Carnival plates exist, and they are outstanding. One flat amethyst Carnival plate is known.

Strawberry Wreath

This pattern displays the best of Millersburg's glassmaking with the finest detailing of the design and the true radium finish. Collectors have found a wide variety of shapes. The easiest color to find is purple, with green and marigold Carnival more difficult. Several examples are known in vaseline Carnival, and another very rare color, olive green, has been reported. Round, tri-cornered, and square bowls are found in various sizes. Large ice cream bowls are rare.

The compote is 3 1/4" tall with a bowl 6" in diameter (the back pattern is Wide Panel). Some of these compotes have one unfinished leaf which is outlined and lacks stippling. I have seen this on examples in amethyst, green, and vaseline Carnival. A rare whimsey compote with sides straight up is known in green and marigold Carnival. These also have the unfinished leaf.

One bowl is known in vaseline Carnival with collar base in a "gravy boat" shape. Some outstanding small odd-shaped sauce dishes are also known. The 5" x 5 1/2" square ruffled shallow bowl is very rare with one each known in amethyst and green Carnival.

Other small sauce dishes are known in amethyst, green, and marigold Carnival. The tightly crimped edges are desired by most collectors.

Swirl Hobnail

Rose bowls, spittoons and vases are known in this pattern. It would be difficult to choose a favorite from these three items. The spittoon would rate highly for shape, color and iridescence. Swirl Hobnail is rarer than Hobnail in all shapes. The rose bowl is known in amethyst and marigold Carnival, but I have never seen a green one. The spittoon comes in amethyst and marigold Carnival, and a green one has been reported. The Swirl Hobnail "whimsey" rose bowl is a larger size. There is no distortion in the glass pattern as normally seen when an example is stretched.

It is believed to have been from the cuspidor mould. Marigold Carnival is the only color reported.

The vases are from the rose bowl/spittoon mould. The colors best known are amethyst, green, and marigold Carnival, but at least one blue Carnival vase exists, too. The blue example I saw was recently found in Northern California.

Tracery

The lone article here is a large, two-handled bon-bon which has a collar base. This come in three shapes: oval, almost round, or square. Its measurements are 7 1/2" by 5 1/2" wide, and there is a plain back with a many-rayed star in the base. The only colors known are amethyst and green Carnival. Amethyst is much rarer than the green, but the latter has better color and iridescence.

Trout And Fly

This has to be one of the most popular patterns by Millersburg, and it is a spectacularly designed Trout. These bowls come in many shapes, including square ones with a variety of edges, in both satin and radium finishes. The ice cream shapes show the fish at its best. To differentiate this pattern from Big Fish, look for the added fly and very minor changes in the water lilies. The known Carnival colors are amethyst, green, lavender, and marigold. Many examples are offered at auctions, but the high desirability keeps a good market value.

The flat plate is rare, with only two known examples in amethyst. One sold at the Doyle auction in 1990. It was damaged, but this did not mar the beauty of the design or the spectacular color.

[Editor's note. Lucille Lowe related this anecdote about Fenton's Trout and Fly pattern in the October 8, 1987, issue of the *Holmes County Farmer-Hub*: "The story goes that John was a great fisherman and was forever sneaking away from the work at hand in the glass plant to make his way down to the Killbuck Creek, where he kept a well-hidden willow fishing pole. A sure indication of Fenton's intentions could be noticed when he would start digging for worms or catching grasshoppers. It is told that Fenton took much ribbing from the Millersburg glass employees about his catches of carp and the forever present bullheads. One day a very jubilant fisherman came galloping into the glass plant with a magnificent big trout dangling on the end of his line. Without a word to all those glasshouse doubting Thomases, he immediately went to his drawing board and designed on of the most sought after patterns in Millersburg Glass today, the Trout and Fly."

Tulip

This rarely-seen compote has been previously listed as an unpatterned Millersburg compote. It stands almost 9" tall, with the unpatterned bowl about 6" in diameter. I have seen amethyst and marigold examples with excellent color and iridescence. This is the same mould as the Flowering Vine compote, but there is no pattern on the interior.

Tulip Scroll

This pretty vase is seldom found. They typically stand 7" tall, but a stretched out version is 11" tall. The known colors are amethyst, green, and marigold Carnival.

Unpatterned

The article in question here is a very rare compote with the same measurements and shape of the Wild Flower. It stands 5 1/2" tall, and the bowl is 6" in diameter. Inside the unpatterned bowl these letters appear: CRYSTAL. Two examples are known in marigold Carnival which have poor color with clear stems and bases. One compote is known in amethyst.

This has sometimes been called the Flute pattern. The term "crystal" has raised many questions. If any one can tell me more about this compote, please contact me. Editor's note: this is probably Millersburg's No. 400 line, which was introduced as a crystal "colonial" pattern in January, 1910.

Vintage

The only examples of this pattern are the 9 1/2" bowls and the small 5 1/2" sauce dishes; all have the Hobnail exterior. This is a simple pattern, but it is so beautiful. The three large bunches of grapes hanging from a wreath of leaves look quite realistic. Add the Hobnail back pattern and a rayed star base, and it becomes a fantastic bowl. Bowls may be ruffled, three-in-one edge, or ice cream shape. Large bowls are known in green and marigold Carnival, and these are the easiest colors to find. Only one three-in-one edge blue Carnival bowl is known. One ruffled amethyst bowl is known. The 5 1/2" small sauce dishes are also rare with one example in amethyst, two each in blue and green, and about eight in marigold Carnival.

Whirling Leaves

This bowl has the Fine Cut Ovals as an exterior pattern. What a variety of sizes and shapes with outstanding colors and brilliant iridescence in satin and radium finishes! The

9" to 10" bowls are known in ice cream shape, six-ruffled, crimped edges, square, tri-cornered, a deep round berry bowl and the very rare diamond shape. The best-known colors are amethyst, green, and marigold Carnival, but three blue examples do exist and four vaseline Carnival have turned up.

Some of these bowls can be acquired at very reasonable prices, and they are nice additions to any collection. The unusual shapes and the blue or vaseline examples are rarely offered, and, consequently, they have a high market value.

Wild Flower

This is one of my favorite compotes. Only an artist could combine eight leaves with eight blossoms and a vine to create a beautiful pattern like the one found on this radium finish compote. Only a few are known in two shapes, the open flared bowl and the deep cupped jelly compote. The latter is 6" tall with a 4 1/2" bowl opening. The brilliant iridescence is found only inside the bowl. The stem and the cloverleaf base on the marigold Carnival compote is almost clear.

The open bowl examples are known in amethyst (damaged), green, marigold, and a single example in vaseline Carnival. I have never seen a jelly compote, but a purple one appeared at a auction in 1985. Both compotes are pictured in Edwards' *Rarities in Carnival Glass* (p. 100). This is one treasured item in my collection.

Wild Rose

Collectors cherish things from the past, and the kerosene lamp represents an important part of living during the time Millersburg glass was being made. It's hard to find a lamp that isn't damaged or with parts replaced. They were used so much that many were bro-

ken. The design consists of a vine with two wild roses and stippled leaves around the base,. These usually have good color and iridescence, and the Wild Rose lamp is a treasure in any size or color.

These lamps were made in three sizes: small, medium and large. Colors are amethyst, green, marigold. More small green lamps are offered, followed by the medium size, with the large lamp rarely seen or offered.

The large Wild Rose lamp is sometimes found with the figures of three ladies on the underside of the base. This is called the Ladies Medallion lamp. These lamps are extremely rare. Only two have been offered at auctions in the past dozen years. Since lamps are usually private sales, it would be hard to estimate a market value. One Ladies Medallion lamp in amethyst sold at an auction in 1989 for $2,200.

Editor's note: An inventory of the Millersburg Glass Co. (dated April 10, 1911) lists several lamps—American Beauty Lamp, Rose Foot Lamp, Rose Lamp, and Mammoth Rose Lamp—but none is described. There is no doubt that the Wild Rose lamp is a Millersburg product, for many fragments were unearthed at the factory. None was found of the Ladies Medallion lamp, however, so there is the possiblity that this is not a Millersburg product.

Zig Zag

This is a plain, but beautiful pattern used on 9" bowls in deep round, square, tri-cornered and ice cream shape. The edges are usually six-ruffled, but some have a plain edge, or a three-in-one or candy ribbon edge. The stippled zig zag rays have a gold iridescence and a radiance of other colors. This has a no pattern on the back, and a 24-point star in the collar base. A little feathered design is between the points on the outer edge. Plain backs are rarely seen on Millersburg, but I have seen a Hanging Cherries bowl with the plain back. Colors known are amethyst, green and marigold Carnival. Has anyone ever seen a blue or vaseline Carnival in this pattern? What finds these would be. A card tray is also reported, but I haven't seen it. A picture was shown in Lincoln-Land newsletter in November, 1980. A 6" marigold Carnival bowl sold at auction in 1978 for $280.

PRIMARY AND SECONDARY PATTERNS

As collectors typically define them, primary patterns in Carnival glass are those made by the plunger during the pressing of the glass. They are also called interior or inside patterns. Secondary patterns are made by the mould, rather than the plunger. They are also called exterior or back patterns, and some refer to them as outside patterns. These definitions are very useful when one is dealing with a bowl that exhibits two patterns.

It's quite remarkable what results when a primary pattern is combined with a compatible imitation cut exterior pattern. John W. Fenton, founder of the Millersburg factory, probably designed the first moulds, such as Hobstar and Feather and Ohio Star, as well as other imitation cut patterns. Today's collectors can collect, enjoy and treasure some fantastic American-made quality glass in either crystal or iridescent colored glass.

When collectors are just becoming familiar with Millersburg glass, they tend to notice the exterior patterns such as Hobnail. This appears on the Vintage bowls and, very rarely, on the Hanging Cherries pattern. On Hanging Cherries, Hobnail appears on some 10" six-ruffled bowls and, even less often, on the 10" ice cream shape and the 6" sauce dish. Colors include amethyst, blue and marigold Carnival.

All Vintage bowls made by Millersburg have the Hobnail exterior, which quickly identifies it as a Millersburg Vintage piece. The many-rayed star on the center base has a small feathered design between each point that encircles the outer edge of the center base. This is known as the Star and Fan, and it also appears on the center base of the Zig Zag bowls and the base of the Tulip Scroll vase. The Vintage and Hobnail combination is found in 9" and 10" bowls in various shapes and edges as well as a 6" sauce dish. All are considered rare with only one known or reported in amethyst or blue Carnival.

The Hobnail pattern also appears on rose bowls, small spittoons, water sets and vases. These are simply called Hobnail and the references to primary/secondary or interior/exterior are not meaningful since there is only one pattern with which to contend! All Hobnail patterns are difficult to obtain and expensive. They can be considered scarce to extremely rare. Any blue Carnival example is a real treasure in any collection.

Some other outstanding examples are the imitation cut patterns. This is understandable since prior to the use of iridescent finishes, some of the finest imitation cut crystal came from the Millersburg factory. On these imitation cut designs, we find a smaller version of the pattern on the center base instead of the many-rayed star (except on Cactus and Country Kitchen). Wide Panel usually has the many-rayed star in one form or another. The ability of John W. Fenton and mould makers not only to create but combine compatible patterns and designs enhances the desirability and beauty, whether it's the satin finish or the radium finish.

Cactus appears on the Rays and Ribbons bowl. Not many comment on this, perhaps because the pattern never gained the popularity it should have. It is an interesting exterior using a variation of the hobstar motif. Rays and Ribbons in the blue and vaseline Carnival colors are top Millersburg rarities, with only two in each color known.

Country Kitchen also appears as a pattern on berry sets; they are almost impossible to locate, but occasionally bowls in various shapes are found. Table sets are rare and expensive. One whimsey spittoon is known and is believed to have been made from the spooner mould. Vases are known, but they are extremely rare. A milk pitcher has been reported. This is another outstanding imitation cut design, whether found in clear crystal or in iridescent glass.

Country Kitchen also appears as the exterior pattern on the Fleur De Lis bowls. The star-like design encircles the outer edge with evenly-spaced imitation cut areas. This presents a very nice design, complementing the already outstanding Fleur De Lis pattern. The Fleur De Lis pattern also appears occasionally as the interior pattern on the Hobstar and Feather punch bowl.

Diamond and Fan is well-known, and it appears as the exterior on the Nesting Swan. It is also one of the most beautiful.

Fine Cut Heart, Fine Cut Ovals and Near Cut Wreath on the exteriors of Primrose, Whirling Leaves and Holly Whirl/Sprig, respectively, demonstrate how various combinations can create a different finished example. These show the artistry of the mouldmakers, whether it is the entire design or a smaller version on the center of the base.

Mayflower, which appears on the exterior of the Grape Leaves bowl, is not very well known and is difficult to locate. It is an intricate design with star-like flowers separated by an unusual diamond and imitation cut sec-

SECONDARY- back or exterior pattern		PRIMARY- interior or inside pattern
Cactus	exterior of	Rays and Ribbons
Country Kitchen	exterior of	Fleur De Lis
Diamond and Fan	exterior of	Nesting Swan
Fine Cut Heart	exterior of	Primrose
Fine Cut Ovals	exterior of	Whirling Leaves
Mayflower	exterior of	Grape Leaves
Near Cut Wreath	exterior of	Holly Whirl/Holly Sprig
Potpourri	exterior of	Poppy
Trefoil Fine Cut	exterior of	Bernheimer/Many Stars
Wide Panel	exterior of	Court House bowl and many other Millersburg pieces

tion. Hold a radium finish bowl to the light and enjoy the beauty, especially the center design. This exterior pattern would have been nice to combine with other Millersburg motifs.

Potpourri appears as the exterior of the Poppy compote with its hobstar, arches and fans. The iridescent luster is exceptional on the Poppy compote, and to see this imitation cut design on the flattened top example is an experience to remember.

Trefoil Fine Cut appears on the exterior of the Bernheimer Brothers bowl, the Many Stars bowl, and the only known Many Stars chop plate. Another known chop plate has no primary pattern, but Trefoil Fine Cut is on the exterior. Trefoil Fine Cut is a well-balanced design with a series of compatible elements. The iridescent rainbow colors, especially the gold and silver hues found on blue and amethyst Carnival examples, prove

the Millersburg factory had no equal in imitation cut patterns.

The Wide Panel exterior on many patterns usually has the many-rayed star in the center base and sharply defined panel lines. This simple secondary pattern, combined with various primary patterns, exhibits a pleasing example especially with the radium finish.

Editor's note: the Wide Panel pattern was probably Millersburg's No. 400 line, which was introduced as a crystal "colonial" style in January, 1910. The court-ordered inventories of the Millersburg plant list many articles which obviously combine the Wide Panel back with a figured plunger: 400 4 1/2" Peacock Berry, 400 6" Peacock Berry Radium, 400 6" Peacock Nappy, 400 8" Peacock Nappy, 400 6" Fish Nappy, and 400 8" Blackberry Nappy. Also listed are 400 Punch Bowls Radium (these are called Flute by Carnival glass collectors today).

CHAPTER THREE

Confusing Patterns

There are so many variations within similar Millersburg patterns that it is necessary to sort out some of the confusion and perhaps to learn how the confusion arose in the first place. The Berry Wreath patterns and the Peacock pattern need to be discussed, and, with careful descriptions, both will become easier to identify.

BERRY WREATH PATTERNS

More questions are asked on how to identify the different berry patterns than any other except the Millersburg Peacocks. It is to your advantage to be able to sort out these examples. There is a difference in the market value, the desirability and the availability—all of which are important, whether you are the buyer, the seller or simply a collector.

The unique ability of John W. Fenton to use a pattern idea with variations is demonstrated in the Blackberry Wreath, the Blackberry Wreath Variant, the Grape Wreath and Grape Wreath Variant, the Strawberry Wreath and the Grape Leaves.

One feature found in all examples is the square-shaped wreath composed of leaves and tendrils with berries extending toward the center in all sizes or shapes of these berry patterns. The design in the center of the wreath will identify each particular berry wreath pattern. What sets the Strawberry Wreath apart is that there is no center design at all. All the wreath patterns have the Wide Panel back pattern, but the Grape Leaves

This wreath design appears in all the berry wreath patterns; see later drawings for the various center details.

bowl does not. It has an intaglio pattern known as Mayflower on the back.

With descriptions of each pattern and illustrations of the centers, you will be able to identify each pattern. The first illustration shown is the square wreath found on all examples of the patterns.

Blackberry Wreath

The Blackberry Wreath is seen more often and in more shapes and sizes of bowls than any of the other patterns. I have wondered why we don't see table sets in this pattern

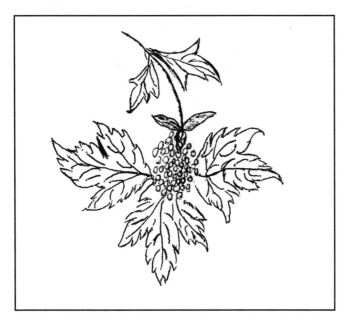

Typical center pattern for Blackberry Wreath pieces.

This center pattern is seldom seen in Blackberry Wreath pieces.

since they were popular items when this glass was being made.

The center pattern that is usually seen is a stemmed single berry with cap, surrounded by three leaves extending from the square wreath. Earlier, this has been the only center design that was reported in articles. There is, however, another center design which is rarely seen. In fact I have only seen two or three examples with this design. In a Columbus, Ohio auction in 1994, one was offered for sale. I was happy to get this bowl for my collection.

Again we see the square wreath; in center of the bowl, a large berry with caps is surrounded by <u>four</u> leaves (not all the same size). Please notice the difference in designs in the illustrations.

The bowl I purchased is a rather deep, square berry bowl 9" in diameter with a tightly crimped edge in a dark marigold color with radium finish. Should this be called a variant? Since we don't known which design was made first, I will refer to it as a variation of the center design for now.

In the blackberry motifs, fewer radium examples are found, but satin pieces are also desirable. The shapes known include berry sets, large and small ice cream shaped bowls, and a variety of bowls in sizes 5" to 10" in diameter with different shapes and edges. Colors are amethyst, blue, green, and marigold Carnival. Not all colors are found in every example. Usually examples in amethyst and green Carnival are seen more often than marigold examples. Details on blue pieces will be covered in a later chapter.

One 8" plate is known in green Carnival. Amethyst and marigold 6" flat plates are known and are classified as rare. Two amethyst Carnival chop plates are known, and one marigold chop plate is reported. An extremely rare spittoon whimsey has been reported in marigold Carnival glass.

Grape Wreath/Grape Wreath Variant

Which is the Grape Wreath? The example with the four-pointed, feathered leaf as the center design in the square wreath was called Grape Wreath in the series of Hartung's books (book 2, page 111). At the time, this was the guide collectors used to identify patterns and names. Later, collectors became more selective, saw more glass and noticed the slightest variations in a pattern. With Millersburg, there's a wide selection. As a result, the term Variant was added to the pattern name.

There are three other center designs known in Grape Wreath Variant examples. These are a clover and feather design and an eight-point star which is sometimes also called a spider web. Another that is rarely seen is a four-pointed star and bars design, which some also call a stylized sunburst.

If these were from the same designer and the plunger determines the interior pattern, does anyone know which are the true variants? Your comments are welcome, since I have failed in finding answers here.

More 6" and 8" bowls with ruffled or candy ribbon edges and ice cream shapes are known than anything else, and they are seen most often. Small sauce dishes and 6" tri-cornered pieces are rarely seen, and they command higher prices. The deep berry bowl and the large ice cream bowls are also rare. Plates are reported, but I have not seen any to date:

The colors known include amethyst, green and marigold Carnival. The Grape Wreath and Grape Wreath Variant patterns probably rate between the Blackberry Wreath and the Strawberry Wreath. I've seen more radium finish than satin examples.

Strawberry Wreath

The Strawberry Wreath has the typical square wreath of leaves, with four berries (no caps) and four tendrils extending toward the center on all examples. There is nothing in

This four-pointed, feathered leaf is the center design in Grape Wreath bowls.

This clover and feather design may be the center design in Grape Wreath Variant bowls.

This eight-point star may be the center design in Grape Wreath Variant bowls.

This four-pointed star and bars design may be the center design in Grape Wreath Variant bowls.

the center except a small dot, sometimes called a jeweler's dot by collectors. I have been told this is a mark made by the plunger in the glassmaking process.

Strawberry Wreath examples typically have the brilliant radium finish and deep colors—blues, pinks and gold hues—all with excellent detailing of the entire design. The color seen most often can only be called a deep purple Carnival. Green, marigold and vaseline Carnival are more difficult to find, but they are outstanding colors, indeed.

Vaseline pieces are found in several shapes. Round, square and tri-cornered bowls are known in several sizes (both large and small), and some have candy ribbon edges. Several of the 6" tri-cornered bowls have a definite vaseline base, but it becomes much lighter over other areas, showing more of a deep marigold color. Small whimseys and sauce dishes are all highly desirable and have a high market value.

Strawberry Wreath design; note the tiny dot.

The ever-popular compote is a must in every collection. Seen most often are amethyst and purple Carnival, while green and marigold Carnival are more difficult to acquire. The whimsey compotes which have the unfinished leaf (only an outline) are very rare. Two marigold, one green and one vaseline are known in the whimsey shapes. I have also seen the typical shape compote with an unfinished leaf. Large ice cream bowls are extremely rare and rarely offered for sale.

Strawberry Wreath items usually command a higher price than the other berry patterns.

Grape Leaves

The reason for including this pattern here is the similarity of the design to the Blackberry Wreath patterns. A novice collector could fail to purchase this outstanding bowl, thinking it a steep price for a berry pattern. The detailing of the entire center design is superb, and the larger berries do look like grapes. The same square wreath is present. In the center of the bowl, there is a large single berry surrounded by four leaves. This bowl has an exterior or back pattern known as Mayflower. Instead of the star, there is a smaller design of the Mayflower on the base. With a brilliant radium finish and the deep colors adding to the beauty of the back pattern showing through, this is a keeper for any collection.

Only bowls are known in this pattern. Amethyst Carnival is the color seen most often, followed by green, with marigold examples rarely seen. The typical sizes for a bowl is 10" diameter, except for a deep round bowl measuring 8" in diameter. In amethyst Carnival with brilliant hues of blue and gold, this size and shape is extremely rare. At the Jack Wilson auction in 1982, a tri-cornered deep green bowl was shown by a collector, but was not for sale.

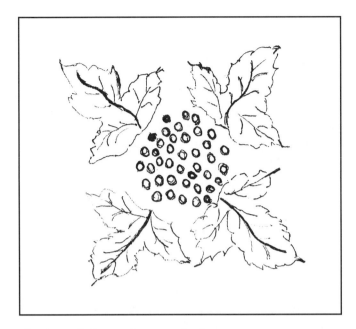

Center of Grape Leaves design.

The vaseline Carnival Grape Leaves bowl is an unusual shape and the only one known in this color. There is a picture of this bowl in Edwards' *Millersburg, the Queen of Carnival Glass* (p. 35). The bowl is slightly damaged, but where is another?

Would you believe this author allowed the vaseline Carnival bowl to get away twice? My only excuse is that I didn't know enough at the time and had the mistaken idea that all examples should be perfect.

This experience is one of the reasons for my desire to separate the berry designs so that collectors can identify each example and know the value of different patterns as well as the availability and desirability of each.

PEACOCK PATTERNS

More questions are asked about this motif than any other. My study of the Peacocks started back when collectors, including myself, were not as concerned about the variations as they are today.

Many stories have been told about the glassmaking era in Millersburg, Ohio. The story about the Peacocks that were seen all around the plant as well as other areas in town is interesting and entertaining. Seeing the live beautiful birds probably had a lot to do with decisions for the many variations of the Peacock pattern. What a choice of shapes and sizes that are available, all super examples in both satin and radium finish.

Because of the vast differences in market value and availability, it's an advantage for the collector to be able to identify the variations. Earlier, there were so many variants that it was easy to get confused. Over the years, names like "Shotgun," "Mystery" and differentiations between Peacock and Peacock and Urn have helped considerably in the identification of these patterns.

I cannot state how many moulds were used for this pattern, since I still have questions unanswered about some of the shapes. Perhaps giving descriptions, sizes, comparisons and ideas that have helped me will make it easier to identify some of the most beautiful examples of Carnival glass.

There certainly were several moulds used for this pattern. I would appreciate hearing from anyone with any additional information about size, shape or color.

Peacock
The Millersburg Peacock has no bee and no beading. Shapes and sizes known in the Peacock examples are the 10" bowls, which include the deep berry bowl, the ruffled bowls and bowls with the three-in-one edge. The three-in-one edge is rare and hardest to find. All have the Wide Panel exterior and the rayed star in the base. The urn has panels

with scallops at the top. The colors found are amethyst, green, and marigold Carnival, with green the most difficult to find. All colors can be found in satin or radium finish. Blue Carnival Peacock pieces are extremely rare; see the chapter on blue examples which lists the numbers that are known and reported.

The ice cream master bowls are hard to find. All are from the same mould, but the measurements range from 9 1/4" to 10" and some are rolled in more than others. Usually, this bowl has an outstanding radium finish and excellent iridescence; on occasion, it is seen with a satin finish. Colors are amethyst, green and marigold Carnival with amethyst being the color most easily found. I have seen fewer marigold Carnival examples, but the amethyst or the green will usually have a higher market value when offered for sale. Blue Carnival examples are also known in this ice cream bowl.

The Peacock rose bowl is extremely rare, beautiful and desirable. These rarely change ownership, and it's usually a private sale. There is one example in each of these Carnival colors—amethyst, marigold and vaseline. I have seen the vaseline rose bowl sell twice at auction.

Like the Peacock rose bowl, the spittoon whimsey (one amethyst and one marigold known) and the banana boat shape bowl (amethyst) are shaped from the large size Peacock bowl. A tri-cornered bowl is also reported in vaseline.

The small 5"-6" bowls are known in several shapes in the Peacock pattern. There is no bee and no beading. The shapes include the ice cream; round deep berry sauce dish; six-ruffled; and rare sauce dishes with the three-in-one edge. The colors are amethyst, blue, green, and marigold Carnival. Not all colors

are known in every shape. More amethyst Carnival examples are known, and the other colors are scarce to extremely rare. In the small bowls, more blue Carnival ones are seen than marigold. Here, rarity has much to do with price. The popularity of these small examples increases the market value.

The piece that collectors call the "whimsey proof bowl" is the same shape as the small deep berry sauce dish: approximately 5 1/2" diameter and 2 1/2" deep. It has no bee, no urn on top of the pedestal, and part of one leg is missing on the peacock. This is rare in amethyst or marigold Carnival, and only one green Carnival example is known.

The Peacock "shotgun" sauce dish has the same measurements as the "proof," and there is no bee, no beading and no urn on the pedestal, but both of the peacock's legs are complete. Colors are amethyst, green, marigold, and it is rare in all colors, especially marigold. In shapes, both the deep berry bowl and the ice cream dish are known.

My theory is that the same mould could have been used for the two examples. We do know that moulds can be altered, which might correct the area where the leg was missing. Another fact is that moulds do wear out. I would never want to see a name change for either, since each simplifies the identification of the examples. I can't help being curious about moulds. If anyone can give an answer, hearing from you would be greatly appreciated.

The small Peacock plate measures 6" d., is very flat, has no bee and has no beading. This is the small berry bowl mould, flattened to make the plate. There are more of the amethyst Carnival Peacock plates known than any other Millersburg plates. Some examples are super, while others lack good color or iridescence. Market value remains generally high, but great increases can be seen when an excellent example is offered. The desirability remains strong among all collectors for Carnival glass plates. More than a dozen such amethyst Carnival plates are known, but just one marigold. Where are the green or blue examples?

Peacock and Urn

Millersburg's Peacock and Urn may or may not have beading on the urn, but the bee is always present. The urn is straight across its top, and it looks more formal than the panelled urn on the Peacock pattern. Peacock and Urn bowls are seen most often, but the giant compotes and chop plates are rarely found.

Bowls in the 9 1/2" to 10" ice cream size are known in amethyst, green, and marigold Carnival, with more in satin finish than the radium. Except for the extremely rare blue and vaseline Carnival examples, green is the hardest color to find in many of the Peacock and Urn patterns. One small ice cream bowl is known in blue Carnival.

Large six-ruffled and three-in-one edge bowls are known, but they are seen less often than the ice cream shape. When the three-in-one edge bowl is offered, it commands a higher market value. The large six-ruffled bowl is known in blue Carnival with either satin or radium finish. Chop plates are extremely rare, and they rank as top items. Amethyst and marigold Carnival examples are known, and they have changed hands in private sales. The marigold has been offered several times at auctions and fetched $2700 in 1992. An amethyst chop plate sold at auction in 1993 for $9,500. At least three amethyst and four in marigold Carnival are known. Is there a green one?

The large Peacock and Urn compote stands 7" high with a bowl diameter of approximately 9." The bowl is 5" deep with a flared, ruffled top, although some are more flared out than others. The pattern has the bee and three rows of beading on the urn. On all of these, the peacock's tiara (horn-like projections on the head) turns forward. There's a variation in the design of flowers with a flower over the leaves on each side of the urn. A very pretty stem on a cloverleaf base enhances the beauty.

The Peacock and Urn compote is real treasure in a collection in any of the known Carnival colors: amethyst, green or marigold. Marigold is the hardest to find, followed by green. Amethyst is seen most often, and it usually has a higher market value. Can you believe a collector bought all three colors at one time? Yes, it happened.

Rumor has it that a blue Carnival Peacock and Urn compote exists, but I have never been able to verify its existence. If anyone has the blue compote, I would appreciate hearing from you.

Peacock and Urn "shotgun" bowl

This 7 1/2" d. bowl was earlier called the Variant. There were many Millersburg variants, so the term "shotgun" was coined. apparently, someone commented that the pedestal without the urn on top looked like the barrel of a shotgun, and this terminology stuck. It makes it much easier to identify this superb example. It has the bee and no urn on top of the pedestal.

This bowl is the same size as the Court House bowl. It has the Wide Panel back and the three-in-one edge. The artistry in the detail of the mould, plus the depth of color and the radium iridescence, make it as one of the best of Millersburg's Peacock patterns. Some of us have been known to count all the tail feathers! With this example, all six rows of tail feathers could be counted, but others have more rows of tail feathers. More green Carnival examples are known, with amethyst and marigold the more difficult to locate. The market value continues moving upward on the "shotgun" bowls.

Peacock and Urn "mystery" bowl

This bowl has two rows of beading on the urn and it has a much larger bee, making it relatively easy to identify. Adding the word "mystery" stopped some confusion. For many years, this bowl was questioned as to which glass company made it. One of the first Millersburg Peacock and Urn bowls in my collection was this bowl in marigold Carnival with a beautiful satin finish and the three-in-one edge. The flowers, the stippled leaves, the detail of the peacock, the Wide Panel back, and the star in the base all suggested Millersburg, but questions remained because of size, the larger bee and the three-in-one edge. These started my close study of the confusing Peacock patterns.

This bowl measures 8 3/4" to 9" in diameter and is rather shallow and flared out when it has the three-in-one edge. I have seen two or three ice cream shapes, and ruffled bowls have been reported to me. The typical Carnival colors are amethyst, green, and marigold, and a few blue Carnival examples are also known. Two different shades of amethyst are known.

Attention was focused on this bowl in 1982 when a blue Carnival one sold at auction for $600. At the Gordon and Charlotte Williams auction in 1988, another blue Carnival example sold for $2,600. Two others sold for $1,100 and $1,700. Some "mystery" bowls are known with good color and iridescence, while others lack the strong color and good iridescence that is most popular in Millersburg glass. The desirability remains high as well as the prices for blue Carnival bowls. In 1993, a blue mystery bowl sold at auction for $2,900.

Peacock and Urn Variant

The term Variant adds to the name of this 6" ice cream-shaped sauce dish. It has the bee, three rows of beads, and the peacock's tiara turns forward. The shape of this bowl is a lot like the Northwood Peacock and Urn. The Northwood Peacock is nicely designed, but details on the feathers and tail are not as well defined as on some Millersburg examples.

The Millersburg Peacock and Urn Varaint has the twelve Wide Panel back and the many-rayed star in the base. The only color is amethyst Carnival with perhaps eight examples known. The market value remains high because of rarity. For me as well as other Millersburg Peacock collectors, it's a "must" because of its differences with other peacock patterns and the existence of only one size, shape and color. A blue or vaseline Carnival example would be a real find. Who knows, one may be out there!

This covers the Peacock patterns as I know them and my ideas for identifying and differentiating among the various examples. One thing I have definitely learned, there was more than one mould used by Millersburg. What a beautiful legacy in Carnival glass for one of the most beautiful of birds. If you can add to this or know of other shapes and size, I would appreciate hearing from you.

CHAPTER FOUR

Base Glass: Vaseline & Blue

Millersburg glass collectors are always looking for an opportunity to add any article of vaseline Carnival or blue Carnival to their collections. These are rarely offered for sale, and the desirability usually determines the price.

VASELINE BASE GLASS

Many collectors have not seen examples of the vaseline Carnival glass made in Millersburg. All pieces are extremely rare, and, in some Millersburg patterns, only one is known at this time. When any collector has one or more examples of vaseline Carnival, they're usually considered among the most prized items in the collection.

Millersburg vaseline usually shows a yellow base color, but has a distinctive greenish tint. If there is doubt, use an ultraviolet "black" light; the vaseline base glass will fluoresce, even in the pastel examples. In most of the examples, you don't need the black light to identify as vaseline glass.

The following is an update on the Millersburg vaseline examples known to me; a few others have been reported.

Acorn
Compote. Two known, one reported. One sold in 1981 for $1,900; in 1982 for $3,000. At auction in 1991, a super compote sold for $2,200.

Big Fish
Four bowls known; two others reported. Various shapes are known: round deep bowl, square with corners turned down, tri-cornered and banana boat. The rose bowl is also known.

Country Kitchen
Covered sugar bowl (1982 Wilson Auction) known. Two spooners known.

Feather and Heart
The only known pitcher sold for $14,000 in 1994.

Fleur de Lis
9" collar base bowl known.

Grape Leaves
One bowl known. Do not confuse with Grape Wreath pattern. The beauty and unusual shape make it one of most desirable. Slightly damaged, but where can another be found?

Hobstar and Feather

One sugar lid known. Two known punch bowl bases with two more reported. Where's the punch bowl?

Holly Sprig/ Holly Whirl

One banana boat shape reported in 1994. Whimsey

Holly Whirl

Rose bowl. One known. Whimsey

Many Stars

One bowl known with six-pointed star base and three-in-one edge. Sold at auction 1991 for $2,200. Another square bowl is known with a tightly crimped edge; it's now in an Ohio collection.

Nesting Swan

One bowl known.

Night Stars

Card tray. Only one known. Sold at auction in 1991 for $625.

Peacock

Round bowl known; tri-cornered bowl known; one giant rose bowl known. One known banana boat shape bowl.

Primrose

Only one bowl known in vaseline. The shape (whimsey boat shape with a tightly crimped edge) is also rare. Reported as found by Janet Knechtel of Canada. Sold at a Michigan auction 1991 for $3,500.

Rays and Ribbons

Two bowls known, both excellent examples. One bowl is 10" diameter by 4" deep and has a crimped edge. Black light not needed to identify.

Strawberry Wreath

Berry bowl 10" diameter (three known); 7 1/2" to 8" deep bowl with sides straight up (three known). One known domed compote (one leaf is plain and almost tri-cornered). Banana boat whimsey (one known). 6 1/2" bowl (two known). The 6 1/2" tri-cornered bowl is known., and a 9" x 3 1/4" deep bowl is known.

Whirling Leaves

Bowls round and ruffled (three known, two others reported). Square, crimped bowl known.

Wild Flower

Jelly compote (only one known).

BLUE BASE GLASS

When I see any blue examples of Millersburg's Carnival glass, my thoughts are beauty, high desirability and rarity. Blue Carnival is not found in all patterns. Some examples have a deep color and excellent iridescence, while other examples may have a dull, rather pale color and lack the vivid iridescence usually expected in Millersburg glass.

In previous years, the value guide most Carnival glass collectors used for blue was to expect to pay three to five times more than the price of other dark colors. Now, one makes the decision of how much they are willing to pay when a blue Carnival example is offered for sale. The color, shape and condition usually determine the higher market values, but with the rarity and high desirability of Millersburg's blue Carnival glass, this doesn't always hold true.

More blue glass is being turned up, but any and all examples are classified rare to extremely rare. The following is an updated list of the pieces I have seen as well as those reported to me. Others may exist, of course, and I would appreciate hearing about them.

Bernheimer Brothers

Advertising bowl, Trefoil Fine Cut back pattern. For color, iridescence and design, this can be classified as one of the best of the blues. Not as rare as some other items, but high desirability keeps price high.

Blackberry Wreath

Small 7" ruffled bowl. Very rare; two reported in radium finish.

Small 7" ice cream shape bowl. One known, very flat with satin finish.

Large 10 1/2" ruffled bowl. Rare. About eight known. Some have poor color and iridescence.

Large 9 1/2" to 10 1/2" ice cream bowl. Rare. About seven known.

Deep Grape

Compote. Very rare. One example known.

Dolphins

Compote. Rare. Four or five known; some damaged.

Hanging Cherries

6" six-ruffled bowl. Rare. 7 or 8 known.

6" three-in-one edge bowl. Scarcer than the six-ruffled; four or five known.

7 1/2" bowl, three-in-one edge. Very rare (one known; two reported).

Large 10 1/2" ruffled bowl. Very rare. Two known.

Compote. Very rare. One known.

Table set. Very rare. Partial sets reported. One butter lid known. One butter dish with wrong base reported.

Hanging Cherries with Hobnail back

Large ruffled bowl. Very rare; two known (one ruffled, other has three-in-one edge).

Large ice cream bowl. One reported

Small 6" six-ruffled bowl. Very rare. One known; another reported.

Hobnail

Water pitcher. Very rare. One known.

Tumbler. Very rare. Two known.

Table set. Very rare. One complete set with amethyst butter dish bottom. One sugar lid known. One spooner reported.

Hobnail Variant vase

One 13 1/2" vase reported.

Hobstar and Feather
7" x 5" diamond shaped pickle dish reported; one punch cup known.

Honeycomb and Hobstar vase
One known. Another reported.

Little Stars
Small ruffled bowl. Very rare; three bowls known. Another three-in-one edge sauce dish reported.

Large 10" ice cream bowl. Very rare. Only one known.

Many Stars
BowL. Rare. Probably 10-12 known. Good deep blue color and iridescence plus high desirability keeps value high.

Large ice cream bowl. Very rare. One known.

Multi-Fruits and Flowers
Punch set. Very rare. One complete set with 6 punch cups known. One other punch bowl reported. Three bases known.

Nesting Swan
Bowl. Very rare. One example known.

Ohio Star vase
A pair reported stolen from the Hartung collection.

Peacock
6" ice cream shape bowl. Very rare. No bee, smooth edge and satin finish. Two known.

Peacock - cont.
6" bowl, six-ruffled, no bee. Rare. About 10 known. Some have weak color, but all blue examples have a high desirability.

6" bowl, three-in-one edge. Very rare. Three known, two more reported. All the three-in-one edges I have seen have deep blue color and good iridescence.

Peacock and Urn (has bee)
Bowl 9", six-ruffled edge. Very rare. Two known.

Bowl 10", six-ruffled, satin finish. Very rare. Two known.

Bowl 10", six- ruffled, radium Very rare. A super example in blue; one known.

Bowl 10", large ice cream bowl. Very rare. One known.

Bowl 8 3/4" mystery. Rare. Bowl on top of urn, with two rows of beading on urn and a larger bee. Four known, two reported. High desirability and high market value.

6" ice cream shape bowl. Very rare. Two known. Has bee, smooth edge, satin finish

Peoples
Vase. Very rare. One known, another reported in Ohio. I have only seen one.

Primrose
Bowl. Very rare. Three known, each with different edge: six-ruffled, flat cream shape or three-in-one edge. One other example reported, not confirmed.

Rays and Ribbons
Bowl. Very rare. Only one known and another bowl reported.

Rosalind
Compote. Very rare. Only one known.

Rose Column
Vase. Very rare. Two examples known.

Roses and Fruit
Bon bon. Very rare. One known, another reported.

Seaweed
10" ice cream shape bowl. Very rare. One known.

6" ice cream shape. Very rare. One known. Among the most outstanding examples of Millersburg blue Carnival glass.

6" six- ruffled sauce dish. Very rare. One known.

Swirl Hobnail
Vase, 13 1/2" tall. Very rare. One known, two others reported.

Vintage with Hobnail exterior
Large 10" bowl three-in-one edge. Very rarely offered for sale. One known. Deep blue color.

Small 6" sauce dish. Very rare. Two examples known.

Whirling Leaves
Bowl. Very rare. Two known, two others reported. Good examples of deep blue color.

CHAPTER FIVE

Millersburg Rarities

Even before Carnival glass became a popular collectible, some items made at Millersburg attracted almost all the keen Carnival glass collectors. These articles—punch sets and vases—were the top rarities then, and they remain so today. Some Carnival glass collectors have never seen some of these rarities, such as the People's vase.

VASES

Yes, these are generally rare, but the purpose is not to dwell on the rarity, but instead to discuss the the beauty, variations and the historical importance as well as different designs in the moulds. I hesitate when using such expressions as "one of a kind" or "only one known" because new discoveries are showing up. The colors known haven't changed much. I have seen every pattern known, but the account of numbers known is from research in Carnival glass publications plus examples reported to me.

Many vases change hands through private sales. Market values have become a guessing game, and, depending upon how much a collector wants an example, how much he or she is willing to pay. Color and iridescence vary considerably, and damage may be present on some vases. Some damage is from use and some imperfections may arise in the making of the delicate designs. The whimsey vases are the ones made from the rose bowl, spittoon or the spooner moulds. These are also called the "swung vase." The numbers known are very limited, and these are rarely offered for sale.

In the early years of collecting, vases were seen quite often, and they were inexpensive and not as popular as other items in Carnival glass. Originally, they were usually purchased to hold flowers and for color and iridescence to brighten the home. What a change we have seen in the past ten years!

People's Vase

The People's Vase has always been acknowledged as the top Millersburg rarity and, of course, the number one vase. The design and the stories of it being in commemoration of the Amish harvest celebration have created an interest in the history of the vases. [Editor's note: The original factory terminology for the People's vase may have been No. 70 "Vase Holland"].

Auctioneer John Woody has been involved with all of these examples, especially the blue Carnival. I am happy to be able to present the photos of the amethyst, green and blue Carnival examples, through the courtesy of Floyd and Cecil Whitley.

The reported history of the People's vases is very much the same, all appearing about the same time, first sold privately and then later at public auctions. Each has had numerous owners. Each was offered very early to several collectors who declined at the time, thinking the asking prices were too high.

This story on the history of the blue Carnival People's vase was written by Helen James Ward of Olathe, Kansas.

"In 1963, about a week earlier than the Wichita show, the blue vase was displayed at a Tulsa, Oklahoma, antique show and offered at $75. The vase had been offered several times to my parents, Mr. and Mrs. Amey, but the price of $75 seemed exorbitant in 1963. The dealer was Max Penny, who attended high school in Ralston, OK. He was a junior the year I graduated in 1939. The Penny family came from the Ingalls-Stillwater, OK, area where my dad grew up. He knew the family well.

"At a 1963 Wichita, Kansas, antique show, the vase was sold to Mrs. Schrader of Hutchinson, Kansas, for $75. In 1967, the vase was sold privately to John Woody by Mrs. Schrader for $400. On September 9, 1967 (Woody Auction, Douglas KS), the vase was sold to Charles Thrawley of Indiana. At a 1969 Woody auction of Thrawley's Carnival glass, the vase was sold to Mrs. Alice Ferrish of California for $2,700.

"In 1972, John Woody contacted Mrs. Ferrish and purchased the vase again for $4,500 to put it as a leader in a Des Moines auction. In 1973 (Woody Auction, Des Moines, Iowa), the vase went to Jim Mogg for $8,100. In January, 1982 , at another Woody Auction where the remaining rarities of Jim and Marlene Mogg were being offered, the blue Carnival People's vase sold again. It went to a Texas collector for $5,000.

"I needed information on the vase for the Old Timers program at HOACGA [Heart of America Carnival Glass Association] in April, 1987. I wanted to find out where Max Penny had acquired the vase. I contacted our school alumni secretary. She told me she had attended Max's funeral, so I was a year late in trying to contact him, and I've always regretted not trying to get information earlier. I was sorry to hear of his death as well as being too late to get history of vase traced back further.

"In the early years Joe Olson would call and visit, and we always talked Carnival glass since he knew I had been associated with Carnival glass since 1958. Some of his information came from me.

"After the vase brought $8,100 at Des Moines in 1973, my father and I talked about memories of the vase, and the Tulsa show in 1963. He had wondered what would have happened if he had offered $50 for the vase."

These kinds of stories and history keep Carnival glass collecting interesting, almost as much as finding and acquiring the glass. There is another blue vase in the Millersburg area; it was confirmed by O. Joe Olson in 1973. I have not seen this second blue vase. The other blue Carnival vase was a bargain at $5,000. What would be the market value today for a blue People's vase?

There are two amethyst Carnival People's vases known, and both have the ruffled top. I have only seen one of these vases, the other example having been reported to me. In reading the articles written about this vase and from Jack Wilson's "Research Notes," I see that this example was described as the "finest" People's vase known. This second example has never been offered for sale. The amethyst vase I saw was found in Holmes County, Ohio in 1971 by Mrs. Florence Martin, a dealer near Millersburg.

Jack Wilson's "Research Notes" (No. 6) recounted the further history of this amethyst

People's vase, as follows: Mrs. Martin sold it to an Ohio collector for $2,500. In 1974, Mrs. Martin bought the vase back for $4,000 for auctioneer John Woody, who paid her a commission of $400. In 1974, John Woody sold the vase to Ray Wishard for a reported value of $10,000 ($3,000 in cash plus seven water sets). In May, 1977, at the Wishard auction, the vase went to a Texas collector for $5,900. It is now is displayed with two other People's vases.

Only one example of the People's vase is known in green Carnival glass. It was displayed in the Millersburg glass shown at the Air Capital Convention in Wichita, Kansas in October, 1992. This green vase appeared in 1965, about the same time the marigold was first known. It was reportedly sold by a Chicago art glass dealer to the Ken Clarks for $75. In 1974, it sold at the Clark's auction to Delton Kemp for $7,100. In 1977, Kemp sold it to Sam Roebuck for $7,100 at a private sale. In December, 1979, it was sold by Roebuck to a Texas collector as part of a three-piece package—a green Frolicking Bears tumbler, the People's vase and a peach opal Farmyard bowl—all for the rumored price of $30,000.

There is only one marigold Carnival People's vase known. In August,1965, this vase reported as bought by Mrs. Charlotte Allanbaugh at a house sale for $45. In 1967, Mrs. Allanbaugh sold it to Dick Loechinger for $650. In 1968, at a Dayton convention, it sold at auction to Ed Collier for $1,050. In February, 1976, at a Woody Auction in St. Louis for Mrs. Collier, this vase was sold to Jim Mogg for $4,500. In August, 1981, the vase was sold privately by Jim Mogg to a Wisconsin collector for a rumored price of $7,000. Since that time, the collector has moved to West Virginia.

Hobstar and Feather Whimsey Vase

The Hobstar and Feather Whimsey vase is fashioned from the giant rose bowl mould, and it is known as a swung vase. I saw an amethyst Carnival example with beautiful multi-colored iridescence on display at the International Carnival Glass Association (ICGA) convention in 1989 at Elkhart, Indiana. Everyone knows my feelings for this pattern, so you can probably picture my reactions when I saw this vase. After looking at it a dozen times, I asked if I could take a photograph. The Wisconsin collector unpacked it as he was already to leave so I could get a picture of the vase.

Only four of these vases are known to exist. I have never seen or heard of one at public auction. Private sales are very quiet, and they don't happen often. Of the four known, two are amethyst and two are green examples. The market value would almost be impossible to estimate.

Swirl Hobnail Vase

While not as rare as the Hobstar and Feather, this is another example of a swung vase. The mould which was used for the rose bowl and spittoon was used for this vase. There are too many known to call it a true whimsey; it is a swung vase made as regular production. Amethyst Carnival is the color seen most often, followed by green and marigold. There is one blue Swirl Hobnail vase known and two others reported. The height ranges from 9" to11". The large size plus good color and iridescence are factors which make a difference in market value. In recent auction, the prices haven't changed much: amethyst Carnival $185-250; green Carnival $250-350; marigold $150-250. For the rare blue Carnival vases, the market value would be decided by the seller and an eager buyer.

Ohio Star Vase

The Ohio Star vases in either crystal or the iridescent Carnival colors are popular with collectors. The Carnival vases are known in amethyst, green, and marigold as well as white. Blue was probably made, too, and Mrs. Hartung reported two stolen in her ad in the *Antique Trader* following her robbery. There is a swung vase made from the normal vase mould.

The opalescent vase was shown at the Wilson auction in 1982. This is probably the only example of opalescent ever produced by Millersburg. It was green and opal throughout (looking more like slag), but it is beautiful. Since no other examples are known, was this experimental?

The market value of the regular Ohio Star vases has increased in the past few years at public auctions: amethyst $1,000-1,200; green $900-2,200; marigold $500-600. Many of the Ohio Star vases are damaged. These prices are an average of those realized for examples with better color and iridescence without damage. The taller vases are included in these prices. As to the white vase or the Aqua Opal, it would be very difficult to give a price.

Rose Columns Vase

With the choice of the different shapes, designs and the old blown vases by Millersburg, it's difficult to decide which is the most desirable. There is no doubt that the Rose Columns vase ranks near the top. This is a mould-blown vase. It is known in four Carnival hues as well as an amethyst Carnival vase decorated with fired-on red, green and gold coloring. The high desirability of this vase and its occasional appearance at auctions has greatly increased the market value in the past few years. Several of these vases had burst interior bubbles and bad cracks. The vases with good color and iridescence and in mint condition will bring a much higher price. This is quite obvious by the wide range of market values: amethyst $1,000-2,100; green $1,100-3,300; marigold $1,600 (damaged)-2,000.

Only two blue vases are known; one sold at the Wilson auction in 1982 for $8,000 to a Texas collector. The other vase sold at auction in 1988 for $6,500.

The amethyst vase with the fired-on colors sold in 1985 for $3,000. These prices paid for the blue and decorated amethyst may be conservative if they were offered today at auction.

Mitered Ovals Vase

This is also a mould-blown vase. It is rare and, in my opinion, one of the most beautiful pieces of glass produced by Millersburg. These vases are rarely offered for private sale or auction. Of the few times at auction, green Carnival examples were offered more, with only one marigold and one amethyst over the past twelve years. More green vases are known, followed by amethyst. I have only seen one marigold vase. An amethyst example with an open bubble on the side sold at auction (June 12, 1993) for $6,750. For green Carnival, the first known auction price is $3,400 in 1958. At auction in 1990, the price realized was $4,500. A marigold vase sold at auction (August 30, 1991) for $2,200. Since the prices paid in private sales are not always known, these auction prices are the only guidelines we have to determine market value.

MILLERSBURG PUNCH SETS

There are only a few patterns known in the punch sets. Both the Hobstar and Feather and the Multi-Fruits and Flowers are complete sets with punch bowl, base and cups. The Big Thistle and the Diamonds exist only as punch bowl and base; no matching cups have been discovered for these two patterns.

Big Thistle is the rarest of the four punch set patterns known. Only two punch bowls and bases are known. Both sets are amethyst Carnival. One bowl has the sides at the top slightly flared out. The other example's sides are straight up. These are rarely offered for sale. One sold at the Wishard auction in March, 1977, for $5,000. At the estate auction of Robert and Kitty Vining (March, 1992), a Big Thistle punch bowl and base sold for $10,000. It went to a Millersburg collector in Illinois. The other is now in Pennsylvania.

As noted earlier, the Diamonds pattern has only the punch bowl and base, no cups having been reported. Two punch bowls and bases are known; one example is in amethyst and the other in green Carnival. In 1986 at an auction, a marigold Carnival punch bowl with base and six tumblers sold for $1,600. The green Carnival set sold at the Vining estate auction in 1992 for $2,000. It stayed with the Big Thistle set and went to Illinois. One green bowl without base is known. One amethyst base sold in 1990. Two bowls without bases are reported in amethyst Carnival.

The Hobstar and Feather punch set has the punch bowl, base and cups. It is massive and beautiful in any color. All the amethyst Carnival sets I have seen have the tulip top, which is turned in. There is one example with the flared out top reported. The green and marigold Carnival sets have the flared out top. Some bowls have the Fleur De Lis as an interior pattern. The green Carnival sets are the rarest, with only three known, but, curiously, the bases are amethyst rather than green! A green base has never been reported. The marigold sets complete have been offered at auctions, and bowls without bases in green Carnival have been sold. A tulip top amethyst Carnival punch bowl and base were sold in 1992 for $3,300. One blue cup is known. There are also three Vaseline bases known (and another reported), but no bowl confirmed at this time.

Multi-Fruits and Flowers is the punch set seen most often. The tulip top set is rarest. Colors known in the tulip top are marigold and green Carnival, with only one set in blue and one in amethyst. I have seen several sets with the flared tops at auction or in private sales. Green is the rarest in the flared top examples. Bases only are offered occasionally. A marigold Carnival tulip top set sold for $2,800 at the Bullard/American Carnival Glass Association Auction in 1993.

Any of these punch set patterns are top items in a collection.

CHAPTER SIX

Glassmaking in Millersburg

BY JAMES MEASELL

The saga of glassmaking in Millersburg is, in essence, the story of one man, John W. Fenton, and the glass plant he built in the largest town in Holmes County, Ohio. Actually, John W. Fenton was involved with two separate companies, the Millersburg Glass Company and the Radium Glass Company. Both were short-lived and failures financially, but they produced some of the most significant pieces of iridescent glassware (now called Carnival glass) ever made in the United States. Two local newspapers, the *Holmes County Farmer* and the *Millersburg Republican,* contain a great deal of important information about the factory and the various people who were associated with it. The *Holmes County Farmer's* editor, L. G. Barton, was particularly enthusiastic about the Millersburg glass plant.

John W. Fenton was born near Indiana, Pennsylvania, in 1869. Little is known of the first three decades of his life, but his younger brother, Frank Leslie Fenton, entered the glass business when he became a decorator at the Northwood Glass Company in Indiana, Pa., in 1897, shortly after his graduation from high school. Both he and John W. Fenton were employed at the Jefferson Glass Company in Steubenville, Ohio, from 1900 to 1903. When superintendent Harry Bastow left the Jefferson firm to start his own enterprise in Coudersport, Pa., John W. Fenton and Frank L. Fenton went with him, and Frank L. Fenton became manager of the decorating department. The Bastow Glass Company's factory was destroyed by fire in 1904, and the Fenton brothers secured jobs at the H. Northwood and Company plant in Wheeling, West Virginia. A 1905-06 Wheeling city directory lists John W. Fenton's occupation as "decorator."

With a year or so, the Fentons decided to go into business for themselves. They rented part of the Haskins Glass Company in Martins Ferry, Ohio, but glass was not made there. Rather, they purchased glassware items, probably tumblers and pitchers produced by other firms (so-called "blanks"), and decorated them. From all reports, success came quickly, and the Fenton brothers soon determined that they ought to have their own factory to make glass. They considered refurbishing factories in two Ohio cities (Shadyside and Marietta) before deciding to construct a new plant in Williamstown, West Virginia. In Williamstown, John W. Fenton was instrumental in selling newly-platted real estate lots through subscriptions to raise funds to build the glass plant. In early January, 1907, the factory was completed, and the first glass was made.

The Fenton Art Glass Company operated in Williamstown in 1907 with John W. Fenton as president and Frank L. Fenton as general manager and secretary-treasurer. Even though he held the title of president, John W. Fenton had little to do with the plant's day-to-day operations. Frank L. Fenton was the man in charge. Another brother, Charles H. Fenton, was vice-president.

From all accounts, Frank L. Fenton was generally careful and conservative in his business practices, while John W. Fenton was impetuous and a bit on the extravagant side. Some have called John W. Fenton a "promoter," suggesting further that he was effective in the formative stages of a project and very good at attracting investors, but that he became restive when faced with the details of running a business and that he was prone to imprudent expenditures.

The early progress of the Fenton plant in Williamstown was accelerated when the company introduced iridescent ware in December, 1907. This glassware, made by spraying hot glass after pressing with solutions of various metallic salts, created quite a stir in glassmaking circles, and other factories (Dugan, Imperial, Northwood and Westmoreland) soon entered the marketplace with their own iridescent products and pattern motifs. This was the beginning of the major production of what today's collectors call "Carnival glass," and it lasted for about eight years.

A few months prior to the introduction of Fenton's iridescent ware, however, the trade journal *Glass and Pottery World* (September, 1907) reported that the Fenton firm might have been interested in buying or leasing "the idle glass plant [in Byesville, Ohio] and running it in connection with their new factory at Williamstown." This trade journal also linked John W. Fenton to the venture: "A mold shop at Martin's Ferry, Ohio is making a long line of molds which are reported to be for the Byesville factory. Rumor credits John W. Fenton and W. P. Beeson of Williamstown, W. Va.

as leasing the former Brudewald plant on the basis of paying interest and taxes for a term of ten years, after which it will become their property. Meantime, they have an option of purchase."

In the spring or early summer of 1908, John W. Fenton made contact with George A. Schodorf of Wooster, Ohio. Schodorf, in turn, soon enlisted the support of businessmen in Millersburg, which is about 18 miles south of Wooster. A headline in the *Holmes County Farmer* (July 16, 1908) read "Looking for a Location," and the newspaper's story related that an officer of the Fenton Art Glass Company was coming to Millersburg to "look over the ground and confer with our people."

A public meeting was held in the Agricultural Hall on July 16, 1908, and John W. Fenton outlined his plans for a glass factory, extolling the virtues of raw materials in the Millersburg area and painting a rosy picture of the economic benefits which would accrue to Holmes County when the plant was operational with 200 employees. John W. Fenton estimated that $40-50,000 was needed to get the plant in operation. Several committees were formed to pursue the idea, including a delegation of three men—Daniel M. Miller, Dr. S. P. Wise and B. C. Sill—who inspected the Fenton plant at Williamstown in order to view glassmaking operations firsthand. Another public meeting was held July 27, 1908, and interest in the glass plant idea began to spread.

The Millersburg-area businessmen quickly secured an option to purchase land, and plans were formulated to sell lots by subscription. The August 6, 1908, issue of the *Holmes County Farmer* carried a lengthy article on its front page which recorded the thoughts of Dr. S. P. Wise in considerable detail. Dr. Wise quoted Shakespeare ("There is a tide in the affairs of men which, if taken at its flood, leads to fortune"), and he was most enthusiastic about

Groundbreaking for the Millersburg plant (September 14, 1908).

the proposed venture. He argued that the loss of Millersburg's young men to Barberton, Akron and Cleveland could be halted by the construction of the glass plant and that the resulting increase in jobs would benefit Millersburg both directly and indirectly.

Lot sales began in mid-August, 1908, and an advertising notice in the *Holmes County Farmer* (August 20, 1908) made this assertion: "You can readily see that in four mouths with 200 men employed your investment will easily be doubled in the purchase of your lot at present." A front page article in the *Holmes County Farmer* (August 27, 1908), probably written by editor L. G. Barton, made the newspaper's position clear: "There are a whole lot of people that can afford to buy lots, and we have a number of men who have money that can well afford to give this thing a boost, who have not yet seen fit to do so, and there are others who have taken but one lot that can well afford to take another. Put your shoulder to the wheel. Be a booster, not a knocker."

Ground was broken for construction on September 14, 1908. As the building progressed, other investors came forward. John W. Fenton was instrumental in selling stock to several prominent Marietta businessmen,

notably H. W. Stanley, Charles Grass, and A. J. Richards. Stanley and Grass were partners in a prosperous wholesale and retail furniture business, and Richards was a well-established druggist. Frank L. Fenton also owned some stock, but there is no indication that he had any role in the operation of the plant at any time.

Construction proceeded through the remainder of 1908, and Millersburg's weekly newspapers reported progress in almost every issue. The *Holmes County Farmer* (November 12, 1908) noted that the stack was completed "a few days ago and it is a monster, being over a hundred feet high."

John W. Fenton was also involved with the drilling of many natural gas wells in Holmes County during the fall of 1908 and the first few months of 1909. The *Millersburg Republican* (February 25, 1909) reported that Fenton was working with the Killbuck and Millersburg Oil and Gas Company. He was also associated with the Deerfield Oil and Gas Company, and he may have drilled some wells on his own, too. Natural gas was piped from several wells to the Millersburg Glass Company's plant. George Irving's research suggests

Right:
Millersburg Glass Company stock certificate.

Below:
This postcard shows men at work on the foundation, walls and main stack for the Millersburg Glass Company plant in the fall of 1908. Researcher George Irving identified three of the men at the top of the stack—Frank Ferris, Mint Spahr and Herbert Tressel.

that crews of Amish workmen were employed for this purpose.

The plant did not begin to make glass until about mid-May, 1909. Photographs were taken at various times during the building of the plant, and many of these were made into postcards. When complete, the factory was an impressive modern structure, indeed. An undated newspaper clipping (probably from the *Holmes County Farmer*) obtained from the Fenton Museum archives, describes the plant as follows:

... it is said by those in position to know to be the best equipped and most modern plant of the kind in the United States, and being ... of concrete, steel and iron, is fireproof. The main building is 300 feet long, 100 feet wide and 28 feet from floor to roof, the entire floor being of concrete. In this building is located the big 14-pot furnace, the stack of which from the bottom of the foundation to the top is about 125 feet high ... [it is] 27 feet in diameter at the pots and 5 feet at the top. There are also three glory hole furnaces in the west end of this building and two electric tumbler finishing machines, a direct connected 25 horsepower fan motor and electric air compressor. On this floor are six tempering lehrs 6 feet wide and 55 feet long and one decorating lehr 90 feet long. The mold room and mold cleaning department operated by electric motors, a direct connected grinding machine with motor, cutting shop with five cutting frames operated by 5 horsepower electric motors, mold oven with metal carriages, double pot arch with heating pots. The mixing room with batch mixing boxes are also in the main building as is practically all the material and machinery for the manufacture of glassware. There are hundreds of molds for three complete lines besides molds for many novelties. In the mixing room can be found feldspar which comes from Massachusetts, soda ash from Barberton, fluorspar from Kentucky, lime from Tiffin, nitrate of soda from South America, sand from Michigan, [and] imported kryolite, potash, bone ash, black manganese, [and] powdered blue. ...Expert electricians pronounce it one of the finest jobs of wiring that they have ever seen. The castings for molds are being made by Mr. Hinkley of the Millersburg foundry, and Mr. Fenton pronounces them first class in every respect. There is a carload of material in the decorating room embracing an entire decorating outfit of every description. The fuel used is natural gas and that there may no shortage in gas the factory gets its supply from two sources. The Killbuck and Millersburg Gas Company has laid a pipeline into the plant, and Mr. Fenton also has two good producing wells that were piped to the plant last Wed., and each line has a separate regulator. Either line will supply a sufficient amount of gas, and if there should be a break in one line, the other can be used, and there is always a reserve in the big pipes at the factory. Mr Fenton has a sufficient amount of casing on hands to drill four or five more wells which he expects to have completed in a few weeks. The factory is located near the CA and C [Cleveland, Akron and Columbus] railway and has a direct switch what enters between the two buildings, with platforms constructed at a sufficient heighth for the easy loading or unloading of goods."

This postcard shows the completed Millersburg Glass Company's plant.

In January, 1909, one of the trade journals reported on the progress of building at Millersburg, noting that the company intended to feature "crystal tableware" but adding that it also "proposed to manufacture opal and other novelty lines." Although the plant was not yet in operation, several trade journal reports from February, 1909, suggest that John W. Fenton had samples of glassware on display in Pittsburgh during January. These reports referred to the Millersburg Glass Company by name, and one asserted that "a lot of orders have been booked" (*Crockery and Glass Journal*, February 18, 1909).

Could samples of Millerburg's first pattern lines have been made at the Fenton plant in Willamstown, West Virginia? John W. Fenton was still president of the West Virginia firm, of course, but this trade journal report only adds to the mystery: "Record time was made in the construction of the new plant of the Millersburg, O. Glass Co., which will be placed in operation within a few weeks. Last October a crop of wheat was taken from the ground now covered by the factory. The business is under the direct control of J. W. Fenton, formerly associated with the Fenton Art Glass Co., Williamstown, W. Va., and now president of the company. However, there are no business relations whatever between the Williamstown and the Millersburg factories, directly or indirectly. Mr. Fenton will retain the presidency of the Fenton Co., but will devote all this time to the new factory, of which he is the sole owner" (*Crockery and Glass Journal*, February 11, 1909).

Perhaps John W. Fenton had arranged for these glassware samples to be made elsewhere. It is known that the moulds for many early Millersburg lines were made by the Hipkins Novelty Mould Company of Martins Ferry, Ohio. Some Millersburg mould drawings exist which bear dates in April, 1909. Samples could have been made at the nearby Haskins Glass Company in Martins Ferry or at one of the glass houses in Wheeling or Bellaire before the moulds were shipped to Millersburg in time for the start of glassmaking operations there in May, 1909.

In any case, the Millersburg Glass Company was making glass in its new plant by about mid-May, 1909. According to the *Millersburg Republican* (May 20, 1909), glassworkers were recruited from "Cambridge and other points" and four shops were at work. The plant operated with union labor from the outset, and records at the American Flint Glass Workers Union archives indicate that Local Union No. 12 of the AFGWU was chartered at Millersburg on May 21, 1909.

Contemporary reports and those issued even a few months later suggest that only crystal glassware was made at first. The first patterns were probably those known today as Ohio Star and Hobstar and Feather. Incidentally, "Ohio Star" was the original factory name for this pressed, imitation cut glass motif, which also carried the factory's No. 353 designation. The pattern now called Hobstar and Feather was called simply No. 358, and the original name, if any, has been lost to history. Several mould drawings for various articles in No. 358, all dated in April, 1909, have survived.

The Millersburg plant apparently had plenty of orders, and one local newspaper (*Millersburg Republican,* May 20, 1909) said that some "were turned over to the Williamstown, W. Va. plant." A week later, the *Republican* noted that "glass dishware, tumblers etc., are now being made by the thousands each day" and offered these thoughts: "Everybody is proud of our new industry, and well we should be, for it will be one of the best industries ever located in Holmes county. Families are moving to Millersburg so fast no houses can be secured,

Millersburg Glass Company president John W. Fenton and sales manager H. F. Weber posed for this picture in the firm's offices a few weeks before glass production began (the calendar above the desk reads April, 1909).

Above: Fairbanks Morse power plant in the Millersburg factory.

Below: Raw materials in the batch mixing room.

Side-lever presses in the Millersburg Glass Company's main work area; note the ductwork overhead for the factory's "wind" system.

and if you are looking for a good investment, buy a lot in the new addition and erect a new house."

Millersburg researcher Lucille Lowe, who operated Killbuck Antiques for many years and made a specialty of Millersburg glass, recounted the story of her grandmother's attendance at an open house sponsored by the factory in May, 1909, during which Ohio Star toothpick holders were given away. The woman wasn't impressed with the little toothpick holder and so expressed herself. As the story goes, she was given an amethyst Feather and Heart pitcher. The time seems a little early for such a piece, but it's certainly possible.

Under the headline "Glass Plant News," the *Holmes County Farmer* (May 27, 1909) carried this story: "The Millersburg Glass Factory is going along nicely, and new work is now being turned out at a rapid pace. The big plant started out as smoothly as if it had been in operation for many years. Without a hitch in anything. New employees are being hired every day, and it won't be long until every department will be in full operation. The new offices of the company are located at the east end of the building and consist of a nicely arranged suite of three rooms, with a large glass showroom on the second floor. Offices,

VOL. XXX.   No. 1.

CHINA
GLASS and LAMPS

JANUARY 29, 1910.

J. W. FENTON,
Millersburg Glass Co., Millersburg, O.

PITTSBURG, PA.
A WEEKLY JOURNAL for the BUYER

ALL THE LATEST NOVELTIES IN GLASS	MILLERSBURG GLASS CO., MANUFACTURERS OF Plain and Decorated Glassware	TEA SETS WATER SETS LEMONADE SETS BERRY SETS

Millerburg Glass Company letterhead; although some products are mentioned in a general way ("water sets," etc.), there are no indications of any specific colors being made.

etc., are equipped with all modern conveniences. Hundreds of people attended Open House at the plant all of last week and were given Ohio Star toothpicks as momentoes [sic] of the occasion and also witnessed the making of glass for the first time."

This same issue of the *Holmes County Farmer* displayed a photograph of John W. Fenton on its front page, accompanied by this laudatory prose, which was probably written by editor L. G. Barton: "It is with considerable gratification that we are enabled to present to our readers this week the excellent picture of John W. Fenton, the man who engineered, constructed and is now operating the big factory of the Millersburg Glass Co. Mr. Fenton came to Millersburg a few short months ago a perfect stranger. Today he has the good will and esteem of everybody. We know Mr. Fenton, and therefore, take the privilege of writing about him as we believe we know him. He is a plain speaking, blunt fellow with a cheerful countenance, who can say yes or no in such a pleasant manner that you know he means it, that [he] knows every minute what he is talking about and does more than he promises. Not many men are built that way. He is not given over to bragging, but keeps his own counsel and does things and does them well, and has given Millersburg the best constructed, best equipped and most modern art glass factory in the United States, and while

that assertion covers a great deal of territory, it doesn't cover too much. He doesn't wait for things to turn up, but fully alive to every opportunity he puts his shoulder to the wheel and does the turning act himself. Now in the prime of life, he is the best example of an energetic, progressive, far seeing business man, the kind we read about but rarely see, that ever struck Millersburg, and fortune certainly smiled on us when he decided to locate his factory here. He has more than made a good every promise and is entitled to the gratitude of every citizen of Holmes County."

On June 10, 1909, the *Millersburg Republican* reprinted a story from the Orrville *Courier* in which a visit by eleven members of the Orrville Board of Trade to the Millersburg plant was reported. The article described the factory's construction in detail and recounted aspects of John W. Fenton's explanation of glassmaking. The account concluded by noting that Fenton "presented each of his guests a beautiful water set and vase as a souvenir of the visit."

In early 1910, the Millersburg Glass Company put its first iridescent glassware on the market. *Crockery and Glass Journal* (January 13, 1910) provided these details, including the firm's name for its new line: "Radium, the very latest colored glass made, is the creation of

J. W. Fenton, of the Millersburg Glass Co., and is now being shown after several years of costly experiments. It is almost impossible to describe. Prismatic is hardly the word to designate its brilliancy, for it has all the soft colors of changeable silk. This new glass will be made in a complete line of both table and lighting goods. The factory gives promise of being the largest independent plant of its kind in the country."

The most extensive contemporary account of Millersburg's products was offered in the January 8, 1910, issue *China, Glass and Lamps*, and much of it was reprinted in the *Millersburg Republican* on January 13, 1910:

"Notable achievement in the arts and sciences is ever recorded, and the greater the work to reach a desired end, the greater the recompense. That is the condition in which the officers of the Millersburg Glass Company of Millersburg, Ohio, find themselves. President [John] Fenton has been endeavoring for four years to produce the queen of iridescent glass. Mr. Fenton's experiments had been successful to some degree, but it was not until the night of January 4, that he had succeeded beyond every expectation. When the glass glowed and sparkled with a thousand varying tints and shades, glistening like beaten silver or flashing like sodden gold, he and the men eagerly and anxiously clustered around him knew that Radium ware would be a complete and lasting achievement in years. All hands were put to work to prepare samples for the Pittsburg exhibit, and they arrived in time for exhibition late in the week. The ware is made in many shapes and there are two primary colors, but others will come later. When placed on a dark background, it flashed forth such rainbow tints as to excite immediate admiration. Place it on a snowy tablecloth and the effect is delicate and beautiful. Every piece is a wonder. One shows a fish at the bottom. In ordinary work, it is simply a cold, white fish. Under the influence of the Radium glass, it pulstates life. Move the dish and the fish seems to move with it, each scale a flashing glimmering sky of rainbow hue. Never did a monster sport in tropical waters surrounded by greater beauty nor accompanied by prettier lights [editor's note: this description probably refers to either Millersburg's Big Fish or to Trout and Fly]. And so one might go on for any stated time, always telling the beauties of Radium ware, but enough has been said to show that the queen of iridescent beauty has been harnessed with the silken cords of color in this discovery of the Millersburg Company. The company's rooms at the Fort Pitt hotel will be an attractive point for many a buyer before the exhibit ends. Among the new lines to be brought out are punch bowls and vases."

Another trade journal account (*Pottery and Glass*, January, 1910) lends this insight into the nature of the products: "Crystal tableware and irridescent specialties are leading features with the Millersburg Glass Co., the display being in charge of H. F. Weber. The specialty line is being shown in many new shapes, consisting of vases, comports, nappies, berry sets, salads and many other pieces. In the crystal tableware four lines are shown. One is a Colonial pattern, while the other three are imitation cut." The imitation cut lines, of course, would include Ohio Star and Hobstar and Feather. The reference to "colonial" designates a well-established style of plain glassware similar to that of Millersburg's "Flute," "Wide Panel" or unpatterned wares. This may be the plant's No. 400 line. A reporter for the *Millersburg Republican* (January 6, 1910) visited the plant, and his story mentioned "a handsome new line of colonial designs that will be very popular."

The Millersburg Glass Company soon began to place ads in the glass tableware trade publications to draw interest to the new Radium lines. The trade press reporters, in turn, responded with increasing coverage of Millersburg's products, and *China, Glass and Lamps* carried John W. Fenton's portrait on the cover of its January 29, 1910, issue. His accomplishments were chronicled, with some exaggerations and a few inaccuracies, in florid prose:

"J. W. Fenton, president of the Millersburg Glass Co. and [former president of] the Williamstown Art Glass Co., is rapidly becoming an important factor in the glass trade of the country. Mr. Fenton began operations six years ago when he established the Fenton Art Glass Factory at Martins Ferry, O. It was a small concern for glass decorating, and the glass was bought in the open market. The enterprise was successful, and Mr. Fenton decided to broaden the field of his activities. He went to Williamstown, W. Va. where he erected a factory, and, being the head of the company he had founded, put all the energy of his intense nature into the enterprise. Success came at the first, and it has been continued, so that the Williamstown plant and its products are known far and wide. But the glassmaker was not satisfied. He had always believed in the doctrine of get there, and always believed that the only way to reach that end was to work intelligently, but to work. He looked over the map, and noting the town of Millersburg, in Ohio, decided that it appealed directly to him. There he purchased a number of acres of land, cut it up into lots and soon had the entire community talking of his enterprise. The next move was the construction of a steel and concrete factory, the highest development of this construction in the country. No time was lost in producing art glass tableware, and it soon became well known. But the final triumph came early in this year when the long desired color appeared in his finished glass, and he knew he had found something better than ever before produced. He named his product Radium Glass, and already it sparkled and glistened its way into the hearts of the buying public. Mr. Fenton is an honest, straightforward business man, one whose word is a good as his bond and whose knowledge of men and things has given him a leading place in every community where he is known. His advancement has been brought about by his unfailing devotion to his duty to himself and his associates, regardless of what time and labor it has entailed. Such men always succeed."

The above account of John Fenton's activities may strain the credulity of today's readers, but one must remember that trade journal writers and local newspaper editors alike were often so caught up in the enthusiasm for a new venture that they lost their objectivity. And, of course, John W. Fenton could be a very persuasive man! However, there is no doubt that John W. Fenton succeeded in developing a "state of the art" glass plant at Millersburg in 1909. As will be seen, however, there is also no doubt that the two Millersburg-based companies with which John W. Fenton was associated were, ultimately, financial failures.

Throughout 1910, the glass tableware trade publications reported on the well-being of the Millersburg Glass Company. The chief product was, of course, the vivid iridescent Radium glass, which the firm sometimes called "Radiumware." *Crockery and Glass Journal* (April 21, 1910) noted that "the several lines of the Radium glass being offered by the Millersburg Glass Co. have created a demand from the dealers and jobbers that has exceeded the

This photograph was taken in either the decorating or the packing area of the Millersburg plant; the identities of the two women are not known, although George Irving tried for many years to learn their names.

expectations of the company. Since the line has been taken up by the premium users, a heavy business has been booked, while the novelties have found a ready sale among retail buyers. Tumblers are now being offered in Radium glass and have proved excellent for packers purposes."

Researcher George Irving learned that the iridescent Court House bowl was being given away in June, 1910. Irving heard various accounts, with many relating a story to the effect that the bowls were distributed to those who had helped to secure a supply of natural gas for the plant.

In mid-1910, a trade journal report mentioned that Millersburg's "berry sets have had a very large sale" and further noted that "the department store and five and ten cent trade have sent in liberal business" (*Crockery and Glass Journal*, June 9, 1910). A week later, this same trade publication called a new pattern "highly meritorious," but offered no descriptions; this account also alluded to a "punch set in a new design" in Radium ware without elaboration.

The popularity of Millersburg's Radium ware continued undiminished in the marketplace, and 1910 was probably a reasonably good year for the firm. The December 8, 1910, issue of *Pottery, Glass and Brass Salesman* broke the news that the Millersburg plant would be expanded and that gas producers would be utilized:

"J. W. Fenton, the energetic head of the Millersburg Glass Co., Millersburg, O., during an interview stated that extensive improvements are under way at the Millersburg factory, which will entail an expenditure of approximately $25,000.

"Walter O. Amsler, of Pittsburgh, has been awarded the contract to install producers at the plant, and he has already begun the work of construction. A new wind system is being installed in the factory, and a tank has been erected. The tank will be placed in blast after the holidays, probably the last week in January. When all the improvements are completed, President Fenton says the skilled force will practically be doubled, as the new arrangement will allow for a much heavier production of ware than heretofore.

"A highly encouraging business outlook is reported, many orders having been booked by the company during the past few weeks. The fame of their line of Radium ware has reached the land of King George, which fact, was attested by the recent shipment of a carload of this well known line to London and Liverpool. Mr. Fenton is much pleased over the trade outlook, and anticipates a steady period of operation at the factory."

Within a few months, however, there were signs that all was not well in Millersburg. The factory was shut down in late January, 1911, about the time a lawsuit between Stephen Hipkins and the Millersburg Glass Company was finally being heard in Holmes County common pleas court. *Pottery, Glass and Brass Salesman* (February 23, 1911) reported that work had resumed on February 6 and further stated that "management report an abundance of orders, enough to keep the factory going for months."

In an interview reported in the March 30, 1911, issue of *Pottery, Glass and Brass Salesman* John W. Fenton was credited with these remarks: "Mr. Fenton stated that the glass industry throughout the entire country was prospering. From every section, he stated, favorable reports are heard and many factories are far behind with their orders. Mr. Fenton, besides being connected with the Millersburg concern, has built many other glass factories throughout the country and was the originator of the present method of producing iridescent glass."

Contrary to some accounts, the Millersburg Glass Company was not closed by a wave of lawsuits filed at about the same time. Stephen Hipkins of the Hipkins Novelty Mould Company had begun legal proceedings against the Millersburg Glass Company and John W. Fenton in August, 1909, just four months after the plant had begun operations.

Hipkins alleged that he had not been paid for the extensive line of moulds with which the firm had made its first products. The Hipkins suit made its way through Holmes County common pleas court, and a hearing was scheduled for January 30, 1911. A judgment was not reached until March, 1911.

Incidentally, architect W. A. Deeker also had had financial problems with John W. Fenton, as this letter (dated February 5, 1909, on stationery from the Schreiber House in Millersburg) reveals: "I came here to look after the settlement of my claim for glass plant plans, as per bill sent you January 15th. I would [have] been glad while here to have taken the matter up with Mr. J. W. Fenton and got a settlement without resorting to the process of law. I have done the necessary preliminary work here for the filing of said bill for collection. If I do not hear from you within 8 or 10 days from the date of this writing, all business that I may have with you after that date will be through my attorney." The outcome of this matter is not known, but no suit was filed on Deeker's behalf.

The case of Hipkins vs. the Millersburg Glass Company and John W. Fenton proceeded slowly as motions and briefs were filed. Court sessions were held in January and February, 1911, and, finally, on March 14, 1911, a verdict was rendered in Hipkins' favor. By this time, many other creditors had also taken legal action against the Millersburg Glass Company. Among them were the People's National Bank of Millersburg, the Union Bank of Chicago, the American Iron and Supply Company, and Fairbanks Morse and Company. Still more legal actions were undertaken by individuals, many of whom had invested in lots or bought stock in the glass plant. All in all, about two dozen lawsuits were filed against the Millersburg

Glass Company, including one by the Holmes County treasurer's office for non-payment of taxes. Little mention of these suits was made in the two local newspapers.

The Millersburg Glass Company quickly went into receivership, and bankruptcy proceedings soon followed. The *Millersburg Republican* (April 6, 1911) assured its readers that "the receivership was a mutual agreement between all parties concerned" and suggested that the plant would soon be operating "on a sure financial basis." The federal district court ordered a complete appraisal of the Millersburg glass plant, its fixtures and all contents. An inventory reproduced at the end of this chapter was copied directly from the original court records (another inventory, somewhat more extensive, exists in Holmes County common pleas court records and is dated April 10, 1911).

Several attempts to sell the plant in the summer of 1911 were unsuccessful, but Samuel B. Fair finally bought the factory and all of its assets on September 23, 1911, for about $14,000, less than half of the appraised value of $32,500. Fair, who was then the Holmes County treasurer, was described as "one of Millersburg's most substantial business men" and was said to be "connected with some of Millersburg's prosperous business concerns" (*Millersburg Republican,* September 28, 1911).

Interestingly, Fair had been among the original owners of the land on which the plant was built, and he had been involved in natural gas well drilling with John W. Fenton and the Deerfield Oil and Gas Company. Plans were laid to make glass once again in Millersburg.

Fair and several others quickly formed the Radium Glass Company, hoping to recapture some of the luster which had characterized Millersburg's most noteworthy products. Samuel B. Fair was president, and three other Millersburg men occupied various posts: C. J. Fisher, secretary; M. V. Leguillon, treasurer; and Carl Schuler, attorney. The vice-president and general manager was a familiar name: John W. Fenton!

A front page story in the *Millersburg Republican* (October 12, 1911) heralded the formation of the Radium Glass Company and listed the officers as noted above. The story also revealed that Raymond Kimble was to take charge of the mould room and that John Mortz would return from Cambridge to be foreman of the glassworkers. The article said that the plant would depend on gas made from coal (i. e., "producer gas") for fuel, rather than on natural gas.

The Radium Glass Company began making glass about mid-November, 1911, using most of the same moulds which had been employed by the now-defunct Millersburg Glass Company. A few mould drawings exist

Blank check from the Radium Glass Company.

which say "Radium Glass Co." on them [Jack Wilson identified two of the items depicted as the Boutonniere compote and the Rosalind compote]. The Radium Glass Company placed some advertising in the trade journals, but its days were numbered. The market for iridescent ware was highly competitive, and the big wholesale buyers and the jobbers may have been reluctant to place their orders with a firm whose past was marked by lawsuits and a long closure. Inevitably, the Radium Glass Company shut down about six months later in May, 1912.

Millersburg researcher George Irving traced the fate of the many moulds used for glass production. He found that Fair had employed several men, including Frank Miller, to clean up the plant. Miller, who was interviewed by Irving, related that the moulds and other metal articles were sold as scrap metal to Godfrey Ittner, who had a business relationship with the Hinkley Foundry of Millersburg. Ironically, the Hinkley firm had earlier made the castings for many of the glass factory's moulds. Perhaps the phrase "ashes to ashes, dust to dust" applies here, at the conclusion of the short, but eventful life of the glass tableware industry in Millersburg, Ohio.

Despite the collapse of the two Millersburg-based glass companies with which he was associated, John W. Fenton continued to

reside in Millersburg with his family. The Jefferson Glass Company purchased the factory in 1913, and lighting glassware was produced there for a few years on a sporadic basis, perhaps with the help of John W. Fenton. In the fall of 1916, the Jefferson firm shut down the Millersburg plant and consolidated its operations at Follansbee, West Virginia. Later, after the glasshouse fixtures and furnaces were removed and the tall stack taken down, the Flxible Company bought the building.

Miss Grace Fenton, 24, the eldest daughter of John W. Fenton and his wife Quindara Kerr Fenton, died in Millersburg of influenza on December 15, 1918. She was then employed in the Holmes County Recorder's office. In June, 1921, Mrs. Fenton was killed in an automobile mishap just outside of Millersburg.

From time to time over the next decade or so, John W. Fenton's name appeared in the industry trade press, usually in conjunction with some proposed glassmaking venture. In September, 1926, for example, he was linked with a project to erect a modern plant in Eureka, Kansas. A year later, his name came up when the Greenlee firm of Bellaire, Ohio, was rumored to be interested in re-opening the Northwood glass plant across the Ohio River in South Wheeling. Neither of these came to pass.

The Flxible Company occupied the glass plant site in Millersburg for many years.

In the 1960s, Lucille Lowe worked to research the history of Millersburg glass. In an article, she noted its connection with her own family: "My ancestors were among the dozens of investors who lost money when the Millersburg glass plant went into bankruptcy. For a time, it was a no-no to even mention it, but even as small child I loved the beautiful glass that both my grandmother and mother hung onto. We just never talked about it, especially in my grandfather's presence" (*Holmes County Farmer-Hub*, special edition, October 8, 1987).

John W. Fenton, 64, died of heart disease at the home of his daughter in Millersburg on January 11, 1934. His grave is in Millersburg's Oak Hill Cemetery. His legacy—the beauty and mystery that is Millersburg glass—will live forever.

LOT 1 IN BLOCK 17 OF THE GLASS PLANT'S PLEASANT VIEW ADDITION

OF IN LOTS TO THE VILLAGE OF MILLERSBURG, HOLMES COUNTY, OHIO.

-o-o-o-o-o-o-o-o-o-o-

Buildings, consisting of factory, warehouse, machine shop, cooper shop, straw shed, and all buildings of every description on said lot; all fixtures, moulds, presses, motors, machinery, wiring, water pipes and all tools of every description,

The above being appraised at, ...$32,500.00

The following appraised separate on account of dispute:

1 Paper press, ...	$ 50.00	
1 Gas Engine, ...	300.00	
1 Remington Typewriter, ...	75.00	
1 Motor, Blower,& Air Compressor, ...	150.00	$ 575.00

MISCELLANEOUS.

13 Empty Carboys, ...	$ 13.00
7 Carboy's Acid, ...	14.00
Wrapping paper, ...	100.00
Collars for lamps, ...	10.00
Fuel, oil and barrels, ...	50.00
Concrete Mixer, ...	25.00
Lot Flour Spar and Fellspar, ...	125.00
Lot sand, ...	100.00
Soda Ash, ...	75.00
Arsenic, ...	50.00
Potash, ...	15.00
Bone ash, ...	20.00
Misc. Chemicals, ...	25.00
Ground Lime, ...	50.00
Asbestos Board, ...	1.00
Sample room and contents, ...	60.00
Office Fixtures, ...	160.00
Packing straw, ...	5.00
Packing supplies, ...	60.00
Hoops and staves, ...	75.00
Nitrate of soda, ...	450.00
Roofing paint, ...	10.00
Asbestos roofing, ...	50.00
Engine oil and tanks, ...	25.00
Cement,portland, ...	75.00
Coal, ...	200.00
Fire clay, ...	10.00
Lot Fire brick, ...	130.00
Total, ...$ 1,983.00	

MANUFACTURED GLASSWARE PACKED.

```
7 Barrels Goblets,,.....................$ 18.00
14 Barrels Tumblers, .....................   40.00
5 Barrels Celery Boats, ..................    9.00
2 Barrels, Table sets, ...................    4.50
1 Barrel Tumblers, ......................    2.25
10 Barrels Assorted ware, ................   16.90
33 Barrels Assorted ware, ................   90.00
37 Barrels Lamps, ........................   20.00
7 Barrels Comports and Pitchers, ........    7.90
4 Barrels Assorted ware, ................    9.00
1 Barrel Vases, .........................    2.25
1 Barrel Assorted ware, .................     .50
24 Barrels Assorted ware, ................   40.00
26 Barrels Small Salts and tops, ........  109.00
                           Total, .............$   369.30
```

MANUFACTURED GLASSWARE NOT PACKED.

No.	Description.	Doz.	Am't.
101,	7in. Berry,	50	$ 21.35
355,	Comports,	20	11.25
105,	7 in. Berry,	150	84.30
400,	4½ in. Berry,	90	20.25
40,	Vase,	8	2.95
358,	5 in. Jelly,	17	6.30
400,	6 in. Peacock Nappies,	80	29.70
353,	10 in. Vase,	4¼	.19
490,	Violet Bowls,	½	.20
400,	5 in. Berry,	14	3.95
50,	Comports,	10	3.70
358,	8 in. Berry,	4	2.25
400,	5 in. Berry,	34	9.55
400,	4½ in. Berry,	40	9.00
101,	Nut Bowls,	4	1.25
4110,	4½ in. Berry,	8	1.80
400	6 in. Berry,	20	7.40
400,	8 in. Peacock Berry,	10	7.10
355,	7 in. Berry,	16	7.20
49,	Vases,	10	3.70
4110,	8 in. Berry,	10	7.10
4110	in. Berry,	10	3.70
400,	4½ in. Berry,	45	10.10
4110,	8 in. Berry,	4	2.75
411,	8 in. Berry,	2½	1.75
410,	8 in. Berry,	26	18.00
4110,	5 in. Berry,	10	2.70
101,	7 in. Berry,	6	3.35
400,	6 in. Fish Nappies,	15	5.55
400,	6 in. Berry,	120	45.00
400,	5 in. Berry,	50	14.00
42,	Comports,	30	11.00
400	Spoon Trays,	100	28.13

```
                           Total, ...........$   386.52
```

			Brought Forward, ... $ 386.52
No.	Description.	Doz.	Am't.
400,	4½ Berry, ...	100	$22.50
400,	Spoon Trays, ...30		8.10
100,	7 in. Star Nappies, ...	11	6.19
400,	8 in. Peacock Nappies, .110		77.70
400,	8 in. Nappies, ...	150	84.35
4110,	8 in. Cherry Nappies,	75	53.10
106,	7 in. Berry, ...	40	22.50
410,	Dolphin Comport, ...	8	10.87
355,	Comports, ...	25	21.10
500,	8 in. Grape Nappy, ...	40	28.35
107,	7 in. Nappy, ...	46	25.87
71,	Vase, ...	5	4.50
72,	Vase, ...	17	15.30
353,	9 in. Vase, ...	25	16.87
70,	Holland Vase, ...	½	1.25
45,	Sweet Pea Vase, ...	56	12.60
40,	Sweet Pea Vase, ...	21	4.73
400,	Vase, ...	3	.67
115,	Comports, ...	14	7.10
44,	Comports, ...	20	5.63
201,	Pitchers, ...	36	32.40
202,	Pitchers, ...	1	.90
110,	Pitchers, ...	15	17.70
500	pitchers, ...	10	11.82
223,	Pitchers, ...	5	12.94
550,	Punch Bowl, ...	9	30.40
110	Tall Comports, ...	3	2.10
358,	Punch Feet, ...	10	27.00
358,	Punch Feet, Crystal, ..	11	24.75
400,	7 in. Footed Bowl, ...	16	12.60
400,	8 in. Footed Bowl, ...	5	5.60
400,	7 in. Comports, ...	7	3.75
108,	7 in. Nappies, ...	8	4.75
400,	12 in. Bowl, ...	40	67.50
400,	8 in. Bowl, ...	6	3.35
400,	6 in. Berry, ...	15	5.57
400,	5 in. Berry, ...	20	6.30
400,	Celery Boats, ...	18	7.70
400,	Bon-Bon, ...	30	9.45
400,	4½ in. Berry, ...	50	8.44
400,	Hotel Cream, ...	14	3.75
400,	Hotel Sugar, ...	35	9.85
400,	Low Comports, ...	28	7.87
400,	Pickle, ...	10	2.59
358,	Nappies, ...120		20.25
	Lemon Extractors, ...	10	3.70
358,	Creams, ...	50	18.56
358,	Spoons, ...	13	3.65
358,	Sugar and Covers, ...	20	12.15
358,	4½ in. Berry, ...	10	2.02
358,	Sundae, ...	22	4.41
358,	Punch Bowl, ...	3	13.50
353,	Punch Bowl, ...	1	6.30
46,	Vase, ...	8	2.97
400,	Baskets, ...	80	22.50
400,	Handled Olives, ...	11	3.09
	Tumblers, ...130		40.50
400,	Syrup Jugs, ...	1,	.99
400,	4½ in. Plates, ...	5	1.12
400,	11 in. Plates, ...	2	1.45
358,	8 in. Oval, ...	6	1.69
355,	Pint Pitchers, ...	8	3.42
412,	4½ in. Berry, ...	70	15.75
	Total, ...$ 1,312.89		

Brought Forward,......... $ 1,312.89

No.	Description	Doz.	Am't.
400,	Punch Feet, ... 3		$ 3.38
	Punch Bowls, ...3		25.65
353-2,	Pitcher, ...2		3.15
358,	Punch Bowl, ... 2		17.10
400,	Punch Bowl, ... 1		2.25
550,	Custards, ...10		2.80
500,	Butter and Covers, ... 1		.80
500,	Sugar and covers, ... 5		3.38
500,	Spoons, ... 5		2.00
500,	Creams, ... 5		2.20
110,	Butter and covers 24		18.90
110,	Spoon and Creams, ...80		21.50
110,	Sugar and covers, ...22		14.85
400,	Goblets, ... 2		.56
	Lamps stuck on Collars, ...98		42.50
	Junk, ...40		2.25
358,	Custards, ... 8		1.80
400,	Sundae, ...22		4.95
355,	Creams, ...80		22.50
355,	Spoons, ...41		10.12
355,	Sugar and covers, ...18		7.70
355,	Butters, Crystal, ...26		14.60
355,	Butters, Radium, ...22		18.56
355,	Spoon, ..."........13		7.30
355,	Butter, Radium, ... 8		2.56
412,	6 in. Berry, ... 5		1.85
412,	5 in. Berry, ... 3		.85
412,	4½ in. Berry, ...17		3.80
400,	Sugar and Covers, ... 5		2.13
400,	Spoons, ... 2		.56
353,	Sugar Covers, ...20		2.25
353,	Bon Bon, ...36		7.30
353,	Celery Tray, ... 8		4.05
353,	Syrups, ...10		6.75
353,	4½ Berry, ...12		2.03
353,	Bud Bouquets, ... 3		1.12
353,	8 in. Berry, ... 7		4.45
353,	Tooth Pick Holders, ... 5		.73
353,	Custards, ...10		2.03
353,	6 in. Berry, ...21		7.09
353,	Olives, ...27		6.07
353,	Butters, ... 5		3.15
353,	6 in. Square Nappy, ...13		4.40
353,	7 in. Square Nappy, ... 2		1.08
353,	Creams, ... 5		1.13
353,	Sugar and creams, covers,..10		5.40
	Pin Trays, ...100		22.50
355,	Footed Bowl, ...75		64.13
353,	9 in. Vase, ... 2		2.82

Total, ...$ 1,733.92

~ SUMMARY ~

Factory and Factory Site, ...$32,500.00
Raw Materials and Supplies of every description, ... 1,983.00
Manufactured Glassware Packed, ... 369.30
Manufactured Glassware not Packed, ... 1,733.92

Grand Total, ...$36,586.22

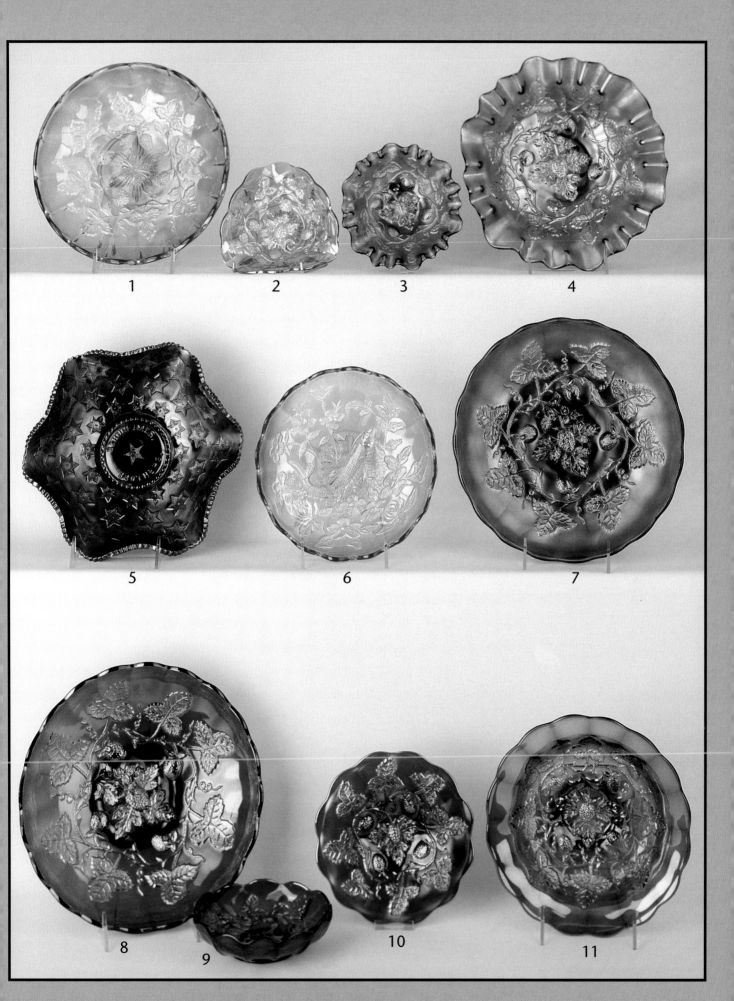

1

2

3

4

5

6

7

8

9

10

11

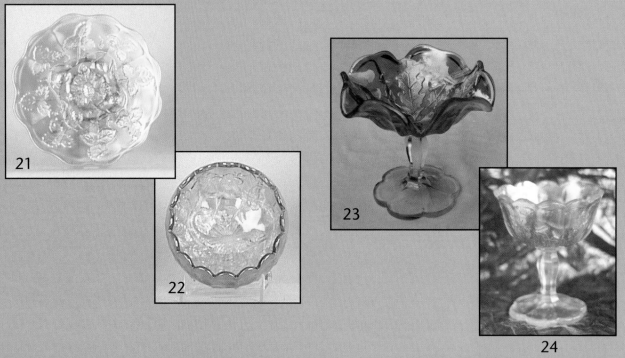

25

26

27

28

29

30

31

32

33

36

37

34

35

38

39

40

99

41

42

43

44

45

50

46

47

48

49

51

52

53

54

55

56

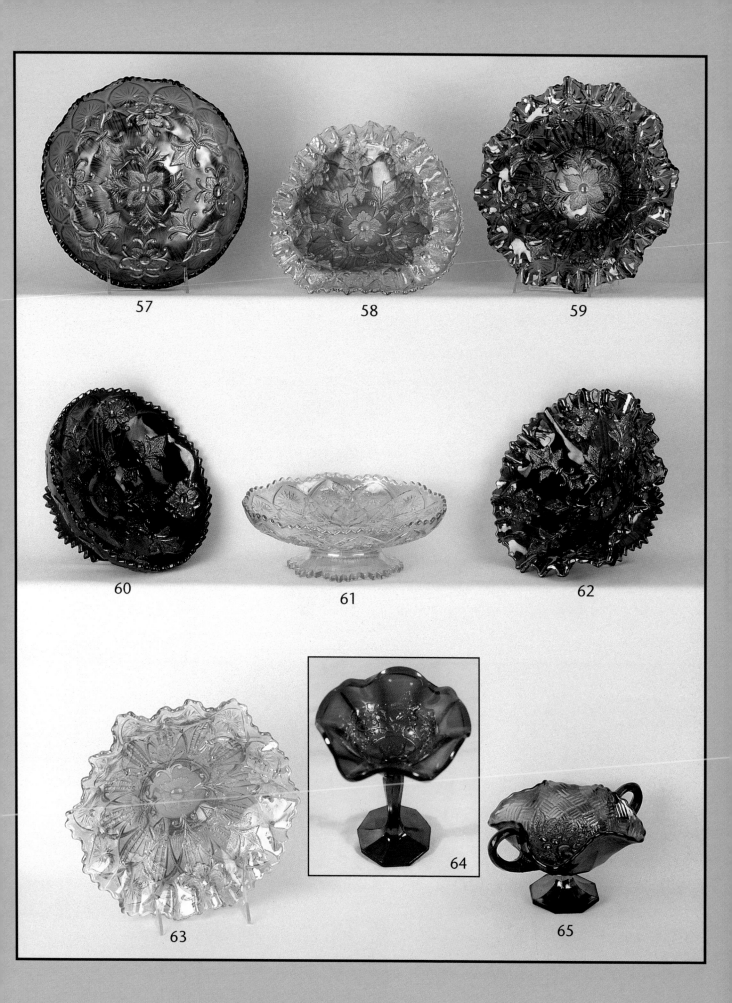

57

58

59

60

61

62

63

64

65

66

67

68

69

71

70

72

73

74

77

78

75

76

79

80

81

82

83

84

85

86

87

88

89

90

91

92

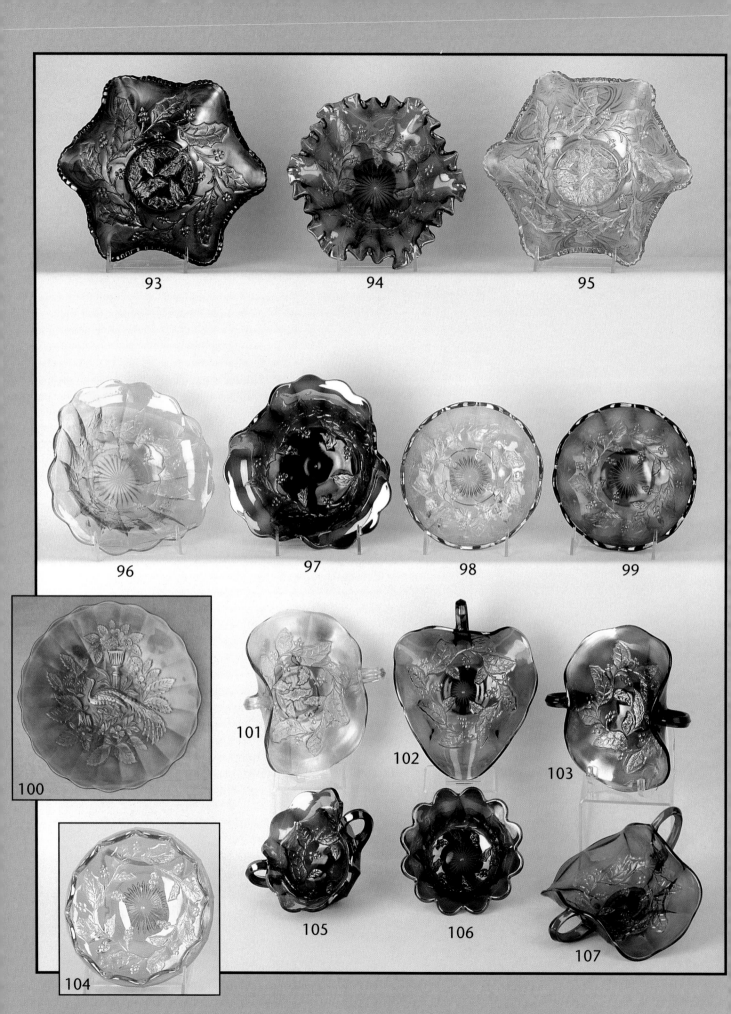

93

94

95

96

97

98

99

100

101

102

103

104

105

106

107

104

108

109

110

111

112

113

114

115

116

117

118

119

120

121

122

123

124

125

126

127

128

129

130

134

132

133

131

135

136

106

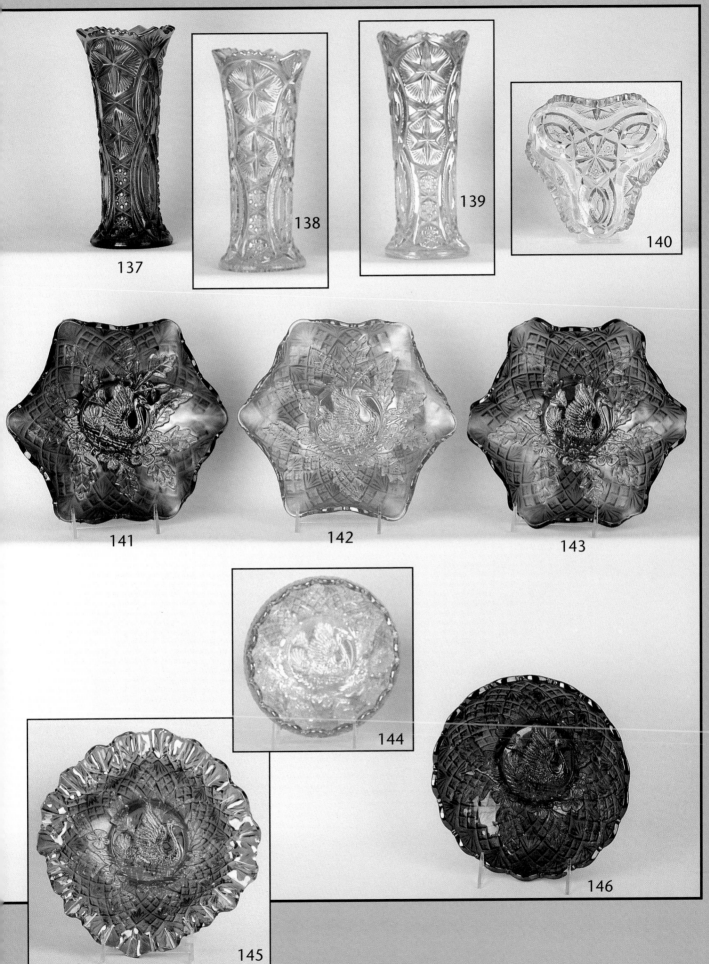

137

138

139

140

141

142

143

144

145

146

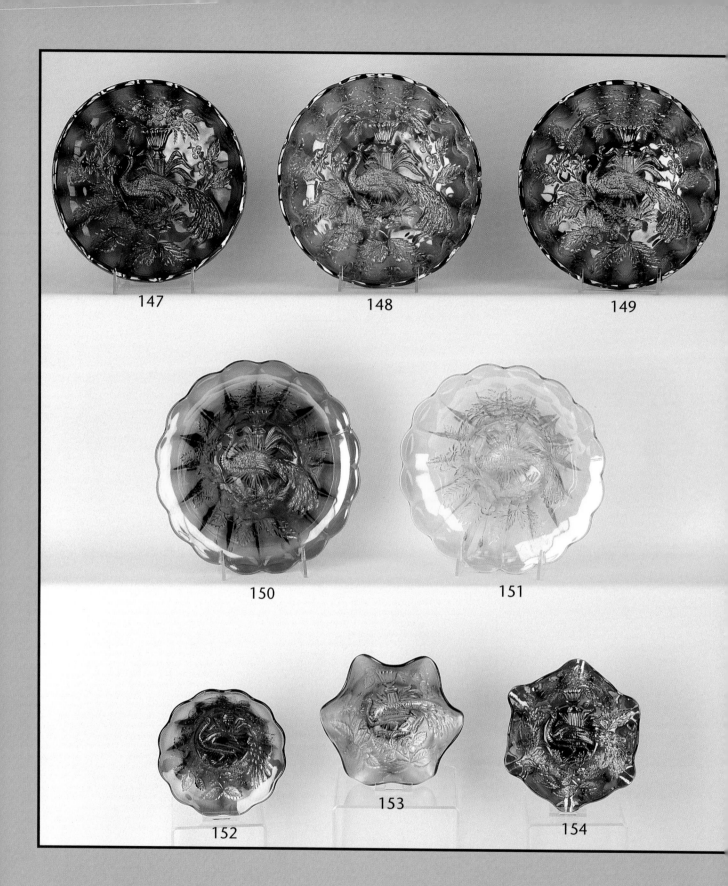

147   148   149

150   151

152

153

154

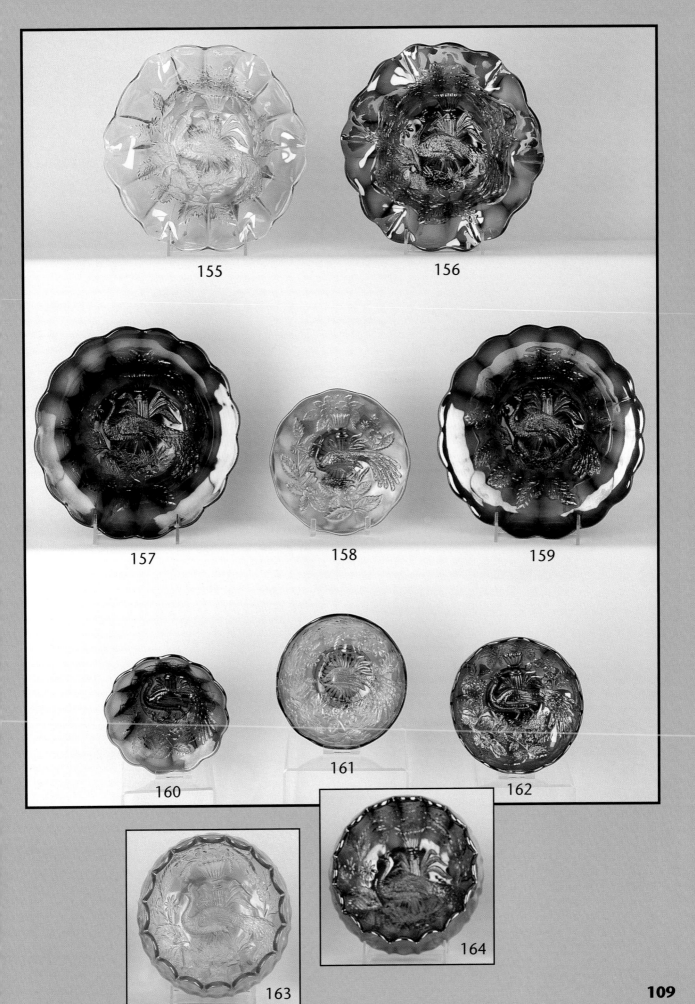

155

156

157

158

159

160

161

162

163

164

165

166

167

168

169

170

171

172

173

174

175

176

177

178

179

180

181

182

183

184

185

186

187

188

189

190

191

192

193

196

197

194

195

198

199

200

201

202

203

204

205

206

207

208

209

210

211

212

213

216

214

215

217

218

219

220

221

222

223

114

224

225

226

227

228

229

230

231

232

233

234

235

115

236

237

238

239

240

241

242

243

244

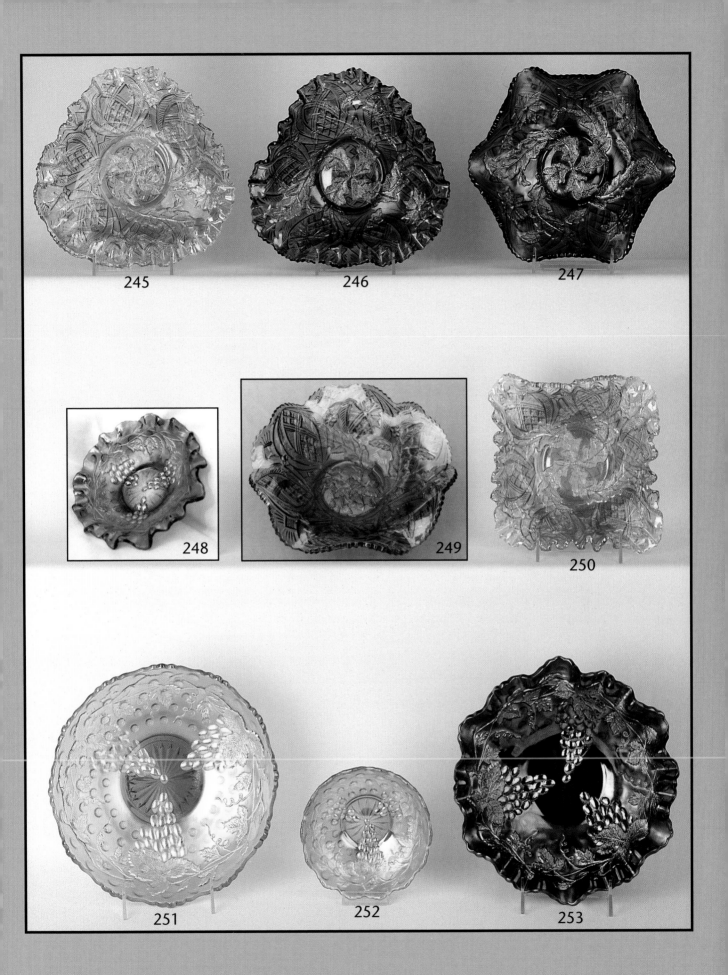

245

246

247

248

249

250

251

252

253

254

255

256

257

258

259

260

261

262

263

264

267

270

266

269

265

268

120

273

275

272

271

274

276

277

278

279

280

280

281

282

283

284

285

286

287

288

289

290

291

292

293

294

295

296

297   298   299

301

303

300   302   304

305   306   307

308

309

310

311

312

313

314

315

316

317

318　　　　319　　　　320

321　　　322　　　323

324　　　325　　　326

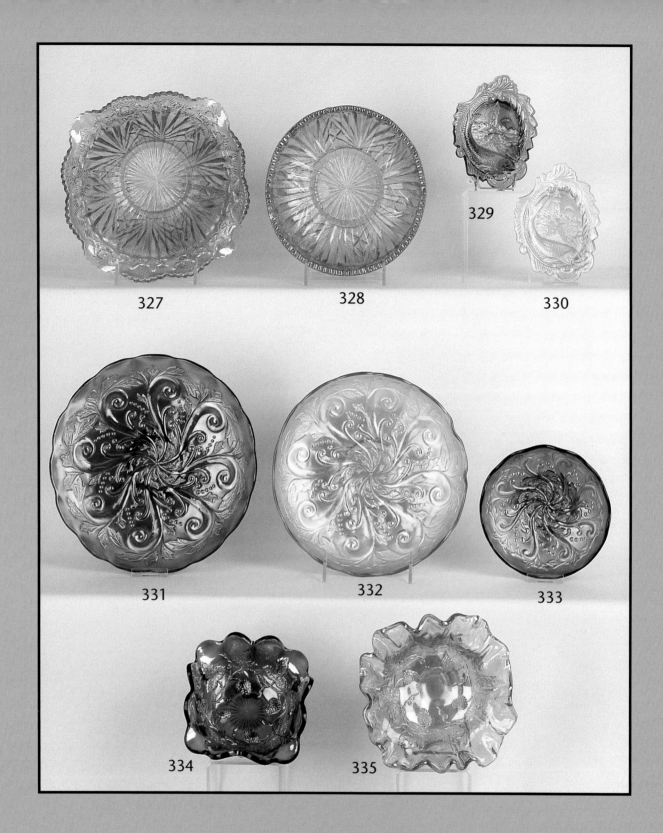

327

328

329

330

331

332

333

334

335

336   337   338   339

340

341   342   343

344   345

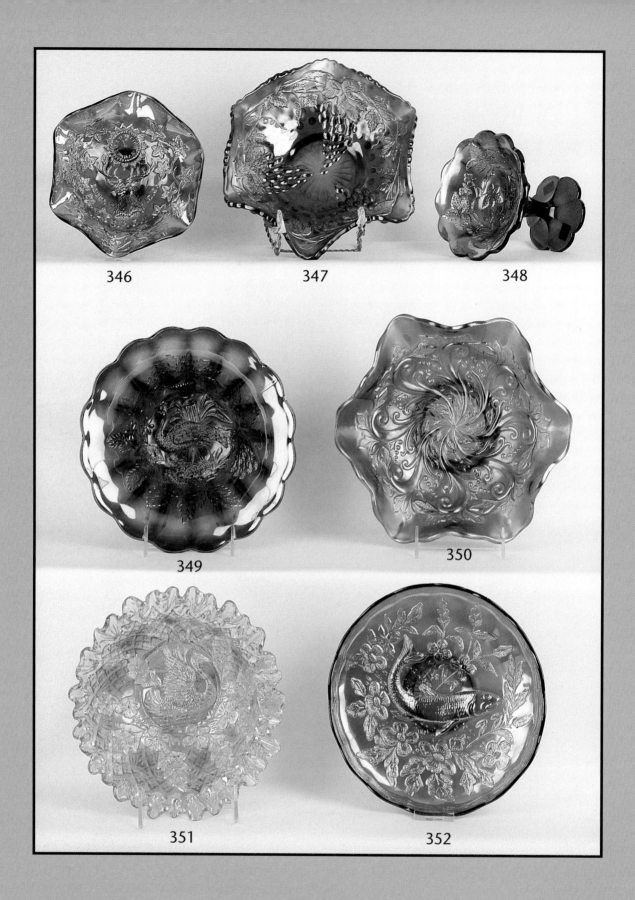

346

347

348

349

350

351

352

353   354   355   356   357   358   359   360   361

362   363   364   365   366   367

368   369   370   371   372

373

374　　375

376　　377　　378

379　　380　　381

382

383

384

385

386

387

388

389

390

391

392

393

394

395

397

396

397

398

399

400

401

135

402

403

404

404

405

406

407

408

409

410

411

412

413

415

414

416

417

418

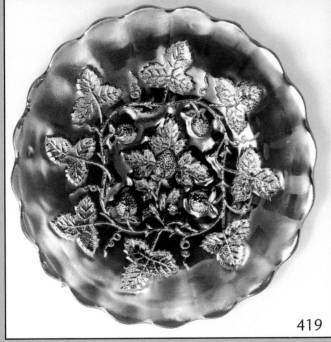

419

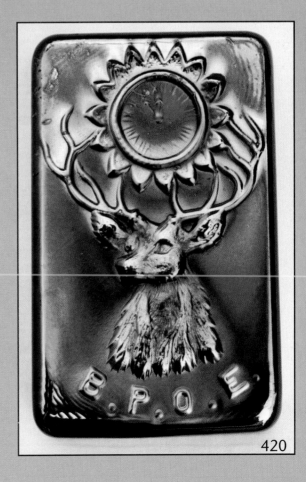

420

139

422

423

421

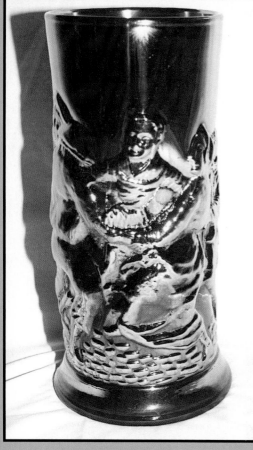

140

424

425

426

427

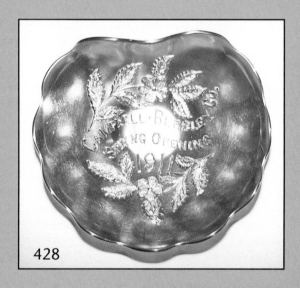

428

430

429

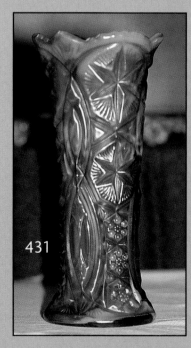

431

432

433

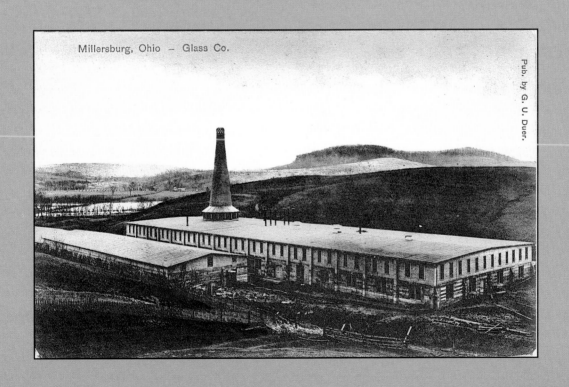

Millersburg, Ohio — Glass Co.

Pub. by G. U. Duer.

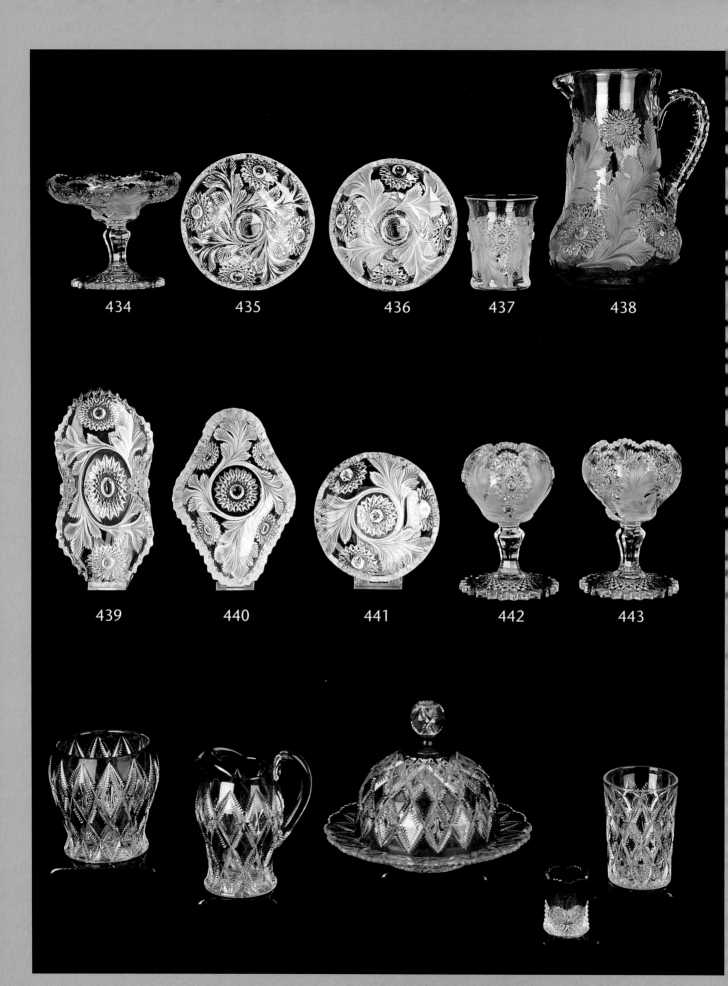

434   435   436   437   438

439   440   441   442   443

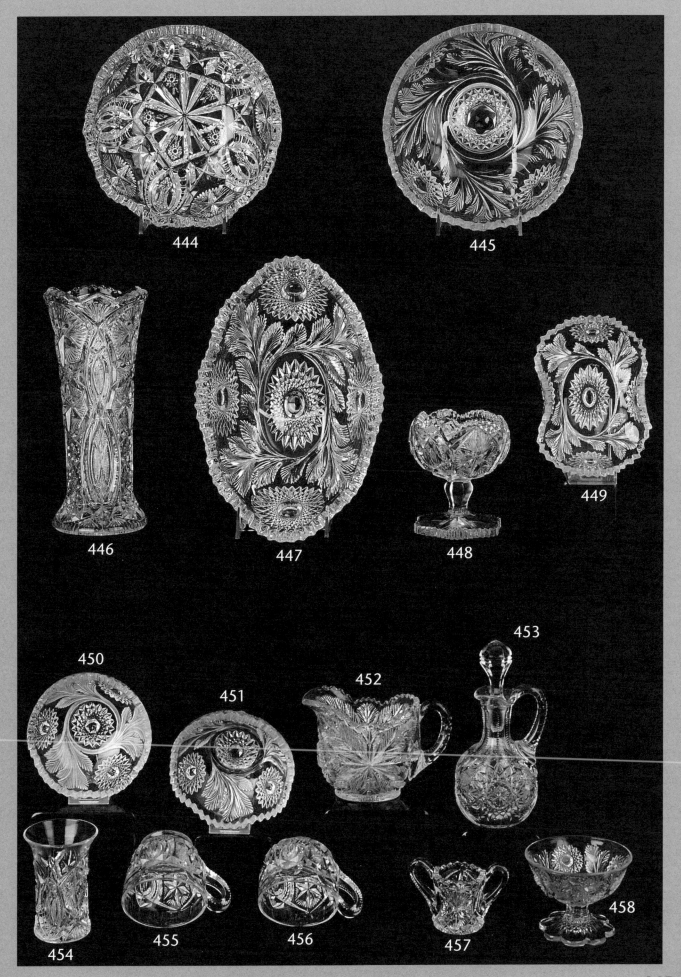

444

445

446

447

448

449

450

451

452

453

454

455

456

457

458

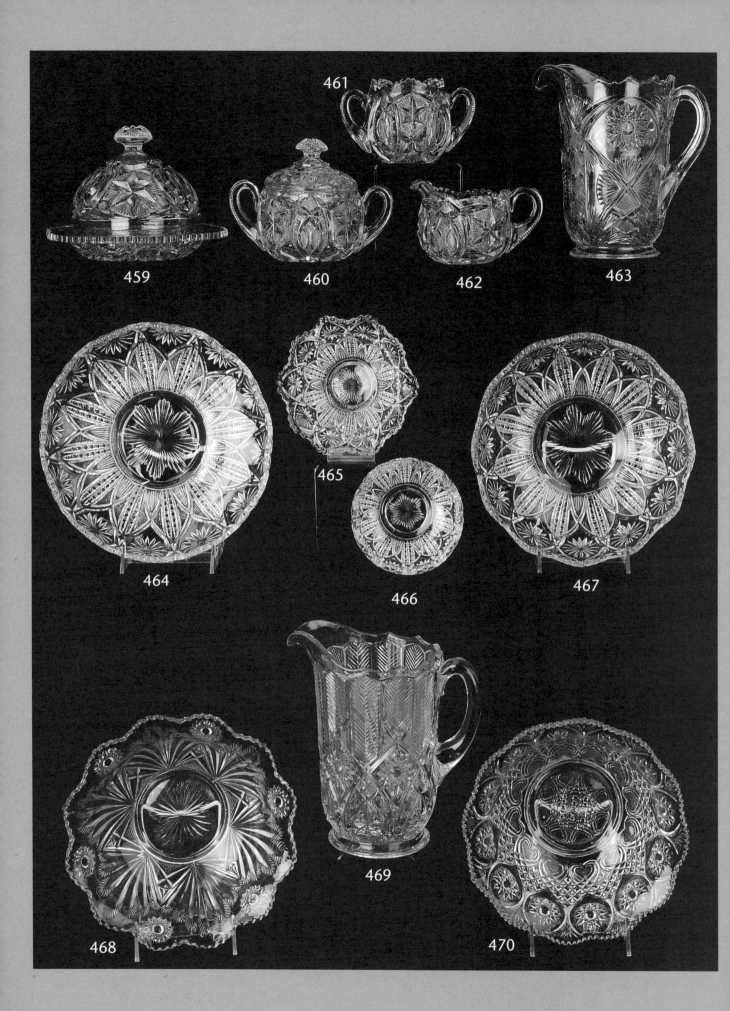

459

461

460

462

463

464

465

466

467

468

469

470

471

472

page 97
1. Marigold Carnival Grape Wreath Variant ice cream bowl. **2.** Marigold Carnival Blackberry Wreath 5" tri-cornered sauce dish. **3-4.** Green Carnival Blackberry Wreath 5" sauce dish and 10" large berry bowl with three-in-one edge (note satin finish). **5.** Blue Carnival lettered Bernheimer Brothers bowl with Trefoil Fine Cut back pattern. **6.** Marigold (note radium finish) Big Fish 8" ice cream bowl. **7.** Blue Carnival Blackberry Wreath 10" ice cream bowl. **8-9.** Amethyst Carnival Blackberry Wreath large ice cream bowl and 5" sauce dish. **10.** Amethyst Carnival Blackberry Wreath 6" flat plate with radium finish. **11.** Unusual lavender Carnival Blackberry Wreath 8" bowl with plain scalloped edge (note the radium finish).

page 98
12. Amethyst Carnival Blackberry Wreath 8" bowl with three-in-one edge. **13.** Marigold Carnival Blackberry Wreath 6" six-ruffled sauce dish. **14.** Marigold Carnival Blackberry Wreath 6" sauce dish with tight candy ribbon edge). **15.** Green Carnival Blackberry Wreath (note radium finish) sauce dish with three-in-one edge. **16.** Marigold Carnival Blackberry Wreath (note satin finish) 10" bowl. **17-20.** Boutonniere compotes in a variety of Carnival glass colors: marigold (note radium finish); green (note satin finish); amethyst (note radium finish and the pulled in bowl); and amethyst (note satin finish). **21.** Marigold Carnival Blackberry Wreath 6" flat plate. **22.** Vaseline Carnival Big Fish rose bowl. **23.** Vaseline Carnival Acorn flared compote with ruffled edge. **24.** Vaseline Carnival Acorn compote; this is a jelly compote with a pulled-in, straight-edge bowl.

page 99
All of these items are the Hanging Cherries pattern, which was previously known as Millersburg Cherries. **25-26.** Amethyst and marigold Carnival six-ruffled 10" bowls (these have the Hobnail back pattern). **27.** Amethyst Carnival large ice cream bowl with Wide Panel back. **28.** Blue Carnival 6" sauce dish with three-in-one edge. **29-30.** Marigold and amethyst Carnival compotes. **31.** Amethyst Carnival (note radium finish) 7" bowl with six-ruffled edge. **32-33.** Marigold Carnival deep round sauce dish (5 1/4" d.) and deep berry bowl (9" d.). **34-35.** Green Carnival six-ruffled 10" bowl and 6" round sauce dish. **36-39.** Green Carnival four-piece table set (butter, sugar, spooner and creamer; the butter base is aqua). **40.** Amethyst Carnival 7" shallow bowl.

page 100
41-42. Marigold Carnival Country Kitchen large and small berry bowls. **43-44.** Green and amethyst Carnival Deep Grape compotes. **45.** Green Carnival Deep Grape stemmed rose bowl. **46-47.** Amethyst and marigold Carnival Feather and Heart tumblers; the amethyst tumbler has "St. Joseph, Mich." stenciled on it. **48-49.** Green Carnival Diamonds pitcher and tumbler. **50.** Amethyst Carnival Country Kitchen spittoon. **51-52.** Marigold Carnival Diamonds tumbler and pitcher. **53.** Green Carnival Cosmos 6" shallow round bowl. **54.** Amethyst Carnival Millersburg Court House ice cream bowl (note radium finish). **55.** Green Carnival Cosmos 6" ruffled sauce dish. **56.** Green Carnival Fleur De Lis compote.

page 101
This page shows many examples of Millersburg's Fleur De Lis pattern to display variations in color, size, shape and edges. **57.** Green Carnival Fleur De Lis (Country Kitchen back) 10" ice cream bowl (note satin finish). **58.** Marigold Carnival Fleur De Lis tri-cornered, dome footed bowl (note the brilliant radium finish). **59.** Green Carnival Fleur De Lis 10" berry bowl with candy ribbon edge (note radium finish). **60.** Amethyst Carnival Fleur De Lis dome footed 10" ice cream bowl (Country Kitchen back). **61.** Marigold Carnival Fleur De Lis dome footed ice cream shape shallow bowl. **62.** Amethyst Fleur De Lis deep, 8" dome footed bowl pulled in at top (unusual shape). **63.** Marigold Carnival Fleur De Lis dome footed bowl, flared at top (the Country Kitchen back shows through the radium finish). **64.** Amethyst Carnival Flowering Vine compote. **65.** Amethyst Carnival Fruit Basket stemmed bon-bon.

page 102
66-68. Green, amethyst and marigold Carnival Grape Wreath Variant bowls with eight-point star center design. **69.** Marigold Carnival Hobnail rose bowl. **70-72.** Amethyst, green and marigold Grape Wreath bowls with the four-pointed, feathered leaf center design. **73.** Amethyst Carnival Grape Leaves 10" bowl (note the radium finish and the Mayflower back). **74.** Marigold Carnival Grape Wreath Variant 6" bowl with clover and feather center design. **75-76.** Green Carnival Hobnail pitcher and tumbler. **77-78.** Purple and marigold Carnival Hobnail pitchers. **79.** Amethyst Carnival Grape Leaves bowl (note the Mayflower back pattern).

page 103

80. Amethyst Carnival Hobstar and Feather covered sugar. **81.** Green Carnival Hobstar and Feather giant rose bowl. **82.** Amethyst Carnival Hobstar and Feather 6″ sauce dish. **83.** Amethyst Carnival Hobstar and Feather spooner. **84.** Amethyst Carnival Hobstar and Feather large square bowl. **85-86.** Amethyst and marigold Carnival Hobstar and Feather punch cups. **87.** Vaseline Carnival Hobstar and Feather punch bowl base. **88-90.** Amethyst Hobstar and Feather spooner, covered butter dish and sugar. **91.** Green Hobstar and Feather creamer. **92.** Marigold Carnival Hobstar and Feather small compote.

page 104

93. Amethyst Carnival Holly Sprig 10″ ruffled bowl (Near Cut Wreath back). **94.** Green Carnival Holly Sprig 9″ bowl with Wide Panel back (note the candy ribbon edge and the radium finish). **95.** Marigold Carnival Holly Sprig 10″ ruffled bowl (Near Cut Wreath back). **96-97.** Marigold and amethyst Carnival Holly Sprig tri-cornered bowls (note the Wide Panel backs). **98-99.** Marigold and green Carnival Holly Sprig 6″ ice cream shape bowls (note the Wide Panel backs). **100.** Marigold Carnival Peacock and Urn chop plate. **101.** Marigold Carnival Holly Sprig card tray. **102.** Green Carnival Holly Sprig tri-cornered nappy. **103.** Amethyst Carnival Holly Sprig card tray. **104.** Vaseline Carnival Holly Sprig rose bowl whimsey. **105.** Amethyst Carnival Holly Sprig two-handled, deep bon-bon. **106.** Amethyst Carnival Holly Sprig deep 6″ d. bowl with scalloped edge. **107.** Green Carnival Holly Sprig card tray.

page 105

108. Amethyst Carnival Honeycomb and Hobstar vase. **109.** Little Stars green 7″ ice cream bowl. **110.** Amethyst Carnival Little Stars 7″ ruffled bowl. **111.** Marigold Carnival Little Stars 8″ ice cream bowl. **112.** Lavender Carnival (unusual color) Little Stars 7″ bowl with three-in-one edge. **113.** Marigold Carnival Little Stars 8″ ruffled bowl. **114.** Green Carnival (note radium finish) Little Stars 9″ bowl with three-in-one edge. **115.** Amethyst Carnival Little Stars 7″ ruffled bowl. **116-117.** Green and amethyst Carnival open ruffled and shallow Little Stars bowls. **118-119.** Marigold and amethyst Carnival Leaf and Little Flowers compotes. **120.** Blue Carnival Little Stars ruffled bowl. **121.** Green Carnival Little Stars 7″ ice cream bowl. **122.** Amethyst Carnival Leaf and Little Flowers ruffled compote (note the brilliant radium finish). **123.** Green Carnival Leaf and Little Flowers compote.

page 106

124-125. Many Stars 10″ ice cream bowls in green Carnival (note radium finish) and amethyst Carnival (note the different stars in the centers—six-point and five-point, respectively). **126.** Marigold Carnival Trefoil Fine Cut chop plate (Many Stars back pattern); there is no interior pattern on this chop plate. **127.** Marigold Carnival (note Satin finish) Many Stars ruffled bowl. **128.** Green Carnival Night Stars two-handled bon-bon. **129.** Marigold Carnival (note radium finish) Many Stars bowl with three-in-one edge. **130.** Amethyst Carnival Night Stars card tray. **131.** Green Carnival (note radium finish) Mayan bowl. **132.** Amethyst Carnival Marilyn tumbler. **133.** Amethyst Carnival Multi-Fruit and Flowers sherbet dish. **134.** Green Carnival Night Stars card tray. **135.** Marigold Carnival Night Stars bon-bon. **136.** Marigold Carnival Mayan ruffled bowl.

page 107

137-139. Ohio Star vase in green and two Ohio Star vases in marigold Carnival **140.** Marigold Carnival Ohio Star tri-cornered relish dish or clover-shaped whimsey. **141-143.** Amethyst, marigold and green Carnival Nesting Swan (note Diamond and Fan back) 10″ six-ruffled bowls. **144.** Marigold Carnival Nesting Swan rose bowl. **145.** Green Carnival Nesting Swan square bowl with crimped edge. **146.** Amethyst Carnival Nesting Swan 8″ round bowl (note the brilliant hues of blue and gold).

page 108

147. Amethyst Carnival Peacock ice cream bowl (note radium finish with brilliant hues of blue, purple and gold; there is no bee and no beading on the urn). **148.** Green Carnival Peacock ice cream bowl (radium finish; no bee and no beading on the urn). **149.** Amethyst Carnival Peacock 9″ ice cream bowl (notice the variation in colors among these three pieces). **150-151.** Green and marigold Carnival Peacock large deep berry bowls (both have the radium finish, and neither has a bee or beading on the urn). **152.** Amethyst Carnival Peacock 5″ sauce dish. **153.** Blue Carnival Peacock 5″ ruffled sauce dish (note satin finish). **154.** Amethyst Carnival Peacock 6″ ruffled sauce dish with radium finish. Note that there is no bee and no beading on the urn on any of these examples.

page 109
155-156. Marigold and amethyst Carnival Peacock 9" berry bowls; each has a slightly flared, ruffled edge. **157.** Amethyst Carnival Peacock deep berry bowl with scalloped edge. **158.** Amethyst 6" d. flat Peacock plate (note satin finish). **159.** Amethyst Carnival Peacock deep berry bowl with scalloped edge (notice the different shades of color and the finishes on 157 and 159). **160.** Amethyst Carnival Peacock 5" deep berry sauce dish. **161.** Green Carnival Peacock 5" ice cream shape (note radium finish; no bee, no bowl on urn); this is called the "shotgun" sauce dish. **162.** Amethyst Carnival 5" Peacock ice cream shape sauce dish (note radium finish). **163.** Vaseline Carnival Peacock rose bowl. **164.** Amethyst Carnival Peacock rose bowl.

page 110
165-167. Amethyst, green and amethyst Carnival Peacock and Urn 10" and 10 1/2" d. six-ruffled bowls (these have the bee, but lack beading on the urn). **168-170.** Green, marigold and amethyst Carnival Peacock and Urn 10" ice cream bowls; each has a bee, but no beading on the urn; all three have the satin finish. **171-173.** Amethyst, green, marigold Carnival Peacock and Urn giant compotes; these have the bee and three rows of beading on the urn.

page 111
174-176. Green, amethyst and marigold Carnival Peacock and Urn "mystery" bowls; these are 8" d. and have a larger bee, along with two rows of beading on the urn and the three-in-one edge (the ice cream shape is also known). **177.** Amethyst Carnival Peacock and Urn "mystery" bowl (these are found in both radium and satin finish). **178.** Green Carnival (note radium finish) Peacock and Urn "shotgun" bowl (this has a bee, but no bowl on the urn; it is 7" in diameter). **179.** Green Carnival Peacock and Urn "mystery" bowl shown to compare the different shades of colors. **180-182.** Green, amethyst and marigold Carnival Peacock Tail Variant compotes. **183.** Amethyst Peacock and Urn Variant 6" ice cream shape (this has a bee and three rows of beading on the urn). **184.** Marigold Carnival Peacock spittoon whimsey (no bee or beading on the urn). **185.** Green Carnival Peacock "shotgun" 6" bowl (no bowl on urn). **186.** Marigold Carnival Peacock "proof" 5" bowl (part of a leg on the peacock is missing, and there is no bowl on the urn).

page 112
187-189. Green, amethyst and marigold Carnival Primrose 10" bowls (note Fine Cut Heart backs); typical shape in satin and radium finish. **190-191.** Marigold and green Carnival Poppy compotes (Potpourri back) in shape usually seen. **192-193.** Marigold and green Carnival Poppy compotes with flat open bowl shape. **194-195.** Amethyst Carnival Perfection pitcher and tumbler. **196.** Amethyst Carnival Primrose 8" round bowl. **197.** Blue Carnival Primrose (Fine Cut Heart back) ruffled bowl. **198.** Green Carnival Pipe Humidor. **199.** Marigold Carnival Potpourri pitcher.

page 113
200. Amethyst Carnival Rosalind 10" d. bowl with three-in-one edge and brilliant radium iridescence. **201.** Marigold Carnival Rosalind ruffled bowl. **202.** Green Carnival Rosalind 6" ruffled sauce dish. **203.** Rosalind large ruffled bowl. **204.** Marigold Carnival Rays and Ribbons (Cactus back pattern) with turned-out candy ribbon edge (note that the edge is virtually crystal). **205.** Green Carnival Rays and Ribbons six-ruffled bowl. **206.** Vaseline Carnival Rays and Ribbons bowl with unusual candy ribbon edge (probably double-crimped). **207.** Green Carnival Tracery two-handled bon-bon dish. **208.** Green Carnival Rosalind 9" ruffled bowl. **209.** Marigold Carnival Rosalind jelly compote (note the shape of the bowl). **210.** Purple Carnival Rays and Ribbons 8" round bowl with scalloped edge.

page 114
211-213. Seaweed 10" bowls in amethyst, marigold, and green Carnival (all have the three-in-one edge). **214.** Green Carnival Seaweed ruffled bowl. **215.** Amethyst Carnival Seaweed bowl with three-in-one edge. **216.** Blue Carnival Roses and Fruit stemmed bon-bon dish. **217.** Green Carnival Roses and Fruit stemmed bon-bon dish. **218-222.** Rose Column vases in all five known Carnival glass colors: purple, marigold, green, blue, and amethyst (with fired on red, green and gold coloring). **223.** Purple Carnival Seacoast pin tray.

page 115
224. Amethyst Carnival Strawberry Wreath square bowl with candy ribbon (note radium finish). **225.** Marigold Carnival (note radium finish) Strawberry Wreath ice cream bowl. **226.** Amethyst Carnival Strawberry Wreath shallow sauce dish (note unusual shape and brilliant color). **227.** Vaseline Carnival Strawberry Wreath tri-cornered 6" d. bowl. **228.** Marigold Carnival Strawberry Wreath round punch bowl shape whimsey; the crystal stem and base are not iridized (this has the unfinished leaf with outline only). **229.** Amethyst Carnival Strawberry Wreath open ruffled bowl **230.** Marigold Carnival Strawberry Wreath compote. **231.** Marigold Carnival Rosalind tall open compote with ruffled bowl. **232-233.** Amethyst Carnival Swirl Hobnail spittoon and rose bowl. **234.** Blue Carnival Rosalind tall open compote with ruffled bowl. **235.** Green Carnival Strawberry Wreath whimsey compote with pulled-in shape bowl (note unfinished leaf).

page 116
236. Amethyst Carnival Trout and Fly ice cream bowl (note satin finish). **237.** Green Carnival Trout and Fly ice cream bowl (note radium finish). **238.** Marigold Carnival Trout and Fly ruffled bowl (note satin finish). **239-240.** Green Carnival Trout and Fly six-ruffled bowl (note radium finish) and amethyst Carnival Trout and Fly bowl with three-in-one edge (note satin finish). **241.** Blue Carnival Seaweed ice cream shape sauce dish (5 3/4" d. and 1 1/4" deep). **242.** Marigold Carnival Flute or unpatterned compote (clear stemmed base); the bowl is lettered inside "cry/s/tal". **243.** Green Carnival Flowering Vine compote. **244.** Marigold Carnival Wild Flower compote (note the radium finish with brilliant hues of pink and gold).

page 117
245-246. Marigold and green Carnival Whirling Leaves (Fine-Cut Ovals back) 9" dome footed bowls with candy ribbon edges. **247.** Amethyst Carnival Whirling Leaves ruffled bowl (this has the typical marie, which collectors call a collar base). **248.** Green Carnival Vintage (Hobnail back) 6" sauce dish (note the crimped edge). **249.** Vaseline Carnival Whirling Leaves bowl with open ruffled edge. **250.** Vaseline Carnival Whirling Leaves square bowl with tight crimped edge. **251-252.** Marigold Carnival Vintage (Hobnail back) large and small ice cream bowls. **253.** Blue Carnival Vintage (Hobnail back) 10" bowl with three-in-one edge.

page 118
254. Amethyst Carnival Zig Zag six-ruffled bowl. **255.** Marigold Carnival Zig Zag ice cream bowl. **256.** Green Carnival Zig Zag bowl with three-in-one edge. **257.** Marigold Carnival Zig Zag ruffled bowl. **258.** Marigold Ohio Star compote. **259.** Blue Carnival Hobnail back pattern on Vintage 10" bowl with three-in-one edge. **260.** Green Carnival Wild Rose kerosene lamp (the base diameter is 5").

page 119
261. Marigold Carnival Wild Rose/Ladies Medallion lamp (portraits of three ladies are on the underside). **262.** Green Carnival Hobstar and Feather whimsey vase. **263.** Green Carnival Wild Rose/Ladies Medallion lamp (note the portraits of three ladies on the underside). **264.** Amethyst Carnival Wild Rose lamp (plain underside)

page 120
This picture shows Millersburg secondary or back patterns; the primary or interior pattern typically associated with each back pattern is given in parentheses. **265.** Cactus (Rays and Ribbons). **266.** Country Kitchen (Fleur De Lis). **267.** Diamond and Fan (Nesting Swan). **268.** Fine Cut Heart (Primrose). **269.** Fine Cut Ovals (Whirling Leaves). **270.** Mayflower (Grape Leaves).

page 121
This picture also shows other Millersburg secondary or back patterns; the respective primary or interior pattern typically associated with each of these back patterns is given in parentheses. **271.** Near Cut Wreath (Holly Whirl/Holly Sprig). **272.** Potpourri (Poppy compote). **273.** Trefoil Fine Cut (Bernheimer Brothers and Many Stars). **274.** Wide Panel (Court House and many other patterns). **275.** Plain back (Zig Zag or, rarely, Hanging Cherries).

page 122
276. Vaseline Carnival Rays and Ribbons bowl with candy ribbon edge. **277.** Vaseline Carnival Whirling Leaves square bowl with tightly crimped edge. **278.** Vaseline Carnival Hobstar and Feather punch bowl base. **279.** Vaseline Carnival Strawberry Wreath 6" tri-cornered bowl. **280.** Two views of the rare Vaseline Feather and Heart pitcher.

page 123

281. Blue Carnival Blackberry Wreath bowl. **282.** Green Carnival Big Fish square bowl. **283.** Vaseline Carnival Big Fish tri-cornered bowl **284.** Green Carnival Tracery two-handled bon-bon. **285.** Blue Carnival Seaweed ruffled sauce dish. **286.** Amethyst Carnival Bulls Eye and Loop vase. **287.** Marigold Carnival Blackberry Wreath sauce dish with crimped edge. **288.** Green Carnival Vintage round sauce dish (Hobnail back). **289.** Marigold Carnival Hanging Cherries 6" flat plate.

page 124

290-291. Blue Carnival Hanging Cherries sauce dishes (note the different edges). **292.** Green Carnival Hanging Cherries 8" flat plate. **293.** Marigold Carnival Country Kitchen bowl. **294-295.** Amethyst Carnival Feather and Heart tumbler and pitcher. **296.** Amethyst Carnival Fleur De Lis rose bowl with domed base.

page 125

297. Amethyst Carnival Flute vase. **298.** Vaseline Carnival Hobnail Variant rose bowl. **299.** Amethyst Carnival Hobnail Variant vase **300.** Amethyst Carnival Hobnail rose bowl. **301.** Green Carnival Hobnail rose bowl. **302-303.** Marigold Carnival Hobnail spittoons (note the differences in ridescence). **304.** Amethyst Carnival Hobnail spittoon. **305.** Marigold Carnival Holly Sprig sauce dish with crimped edge. **306.** Amethyst Carnival Holly Sprig bowl with pie crust edge. **307.** Green Carnival Holly Sprig square sauce dish.

page 126

308. Amethyst Carnival Little Star round sauce dish. **309.** Blue Carnival Many Stars bowl (Trefoil Fine Cut back); note the six-point star in the center. **310.** Amethyst Carnival Many Stars bowl (Trefoil Fine Cut back); note the five-point star in the center. **311.** Marigold Carnival Mitred Ovals vase. **312.** Green Carnival Multi-Fruits and Flowers sherbet dish. **313.** Amethyst Carnival Leaf and Little Flowers compote. **314.** Amethyst Carnival Peacock and Urn "mystery" plate (note the bee and the two rows of beading on the urn). **315.** Blue Carnival Peacock and Urn mystery bowl. **316.** Vaseline Carnival Night Stars card tray. **317.** Olive green Carnival Night Stars bon-bon dish.

page 127

318. Marigold Carnival Ohio Star compote. **319.** Amethyst Carnival Olympic compote. **320.** Blue Carnival Peacock and Urn ruffled bowl. **321.** Blue Carnival Peacock round sauce dish. **322.** Marigold Carnival Peacock and Urn ice cream bowl. **323.** Amethyst Carnival Flute compote. **324.** Green Carnival Rosalind compote. **325.** Green Carnival Rosalind ruffled sauce dish. **326.** Marigold Carnival Rosalind round sauce dish.

page 128

327. Marigold Carnival Rays and Ribbons square bowl (Cactus back). **328.** Marigold Carnival Rays and Ribbons rose bowl (Cactus back). **329.** Green Carnival Seacoast pin tray. **330.** Marigold Carnival Seacoast pin tray. **331.** Amethyst Carnival Seaweed plate. **332.** Marigold Carnival Seaweed ice cream bowl. **333.** Amethyst Carnival Seaweed round sauce dish. **334.** Green Carnival Strawberry Wreath square sauce dish. **335.** Marigold Carnival Strawberry Wreath compote with tight ruffled edge

page 129

336. Green Carnival Tulip Scroll vase. **337.** Blue Carnival Swirl Hobnail vase. **338.** Green Carnival Swirl Hobnail vase. **339.** Amethyst Carnival Swirl Hobnail vase (note nine rows of hobnails). **340.** Marigold Carnival Swirl Hobnail spittoon. **341.** Marigold Carnival Swirl Hobnail spittoon (note nine rows of hobnails). **342.** Amethyst Carnival Tracery square bon-bon. **343.** Amethyst Carnival Tulip compote. **344.** Marigold Carnival Trout and Fly square bowl. **345.** Marigold Carnival Trout and Fly ice cream bowl.

page 130

346. Amethyst Carnival Elk ruffled bowl. **347.** Amethyst Carnival Vintage bowl (Hobnail back). **348.** Amethyst Carnival Wild Flower compote. **349.** Amethyst Carnival Peacock berry bowl. **350.** Green Carnival Seaweed 10" ruffled bowl. **351.** Marigold Carnival Nesting Swan round bowl with tightly crimped edge. **352.** Green Carnival Trout and fly bowl.

page 131
353. Amethyst Carnival Morning Glory tumbler. **354.** Amethyst Carnival Morning Glory pitcher. **355.** Amethyst Carnival Multi-Fruits and Flowers tumbler. **356.** Amethyst Carnival Multi-Fruits and Flowers pitcher. **357.** Marigold Carnival Multi-Fruits and Flowers tumbler. **358.** Green Carnival Feather and Heart tumbler. **359.** Green Carnival Feather and Heart pitcher. **360.** Marigold Carnival Morning Glory tumbler. **361.** Marigold Carnival Morning Glory pitcher. **362.** Amethyst Carnival Marilyn pitcher. **363.** Amethyst Carnival Marilyn tumbler. **364.** Marigold Carnival Marilyn pitcher. **365.** Marigold Carnival Marilyn tumbler. **366.** Green Carnival Marilyn pitcher. **367.** Green Carnival Marilyn tumbler **368.** Marigold Carnival Hanging Cherries tumbler. **369.** Marigold Carnival Hanging Cherries pitcher. **370.** Green Carnival Hanging Cherries Variant tumbler. **371.** Green Carnival Hanging Cherries pitcher. **372.** Green Carnival Hanging Cherries tumbler.

page 132
373. Green Carnival Hanging Cherries chop plate. **374.** Green Carnival Multi-Fruits and Flowers punch bowl and base. **375.** Green Carnival Multi-Fruits and Flowers punch cup. **376.** Amethyst Carnival Zig Zag bowl. **377.** Amethyst Carnival Seaweed bowl (collar base). **378.** Amethyst Carnival Dolphin compote with Rosalind interior (see also Fig. 387). **379.** Vaseline Carnival Fleur De Lis square bowl with Country Kitchen exterior (dome foot). **380.** Green Carnival Big Fish triangular bowl (note radium finish). **381.** Vaseline Carnival Strawberry Wreath square bowl.

page 133
382. Green Carnival Acorn compote. **383.** Blue Carnival Whirling Leaves bowl with three-in-one edge. **384.** Green Carnival Nesting Swan bowl (this is called the "mould-shape" bowl by collectors). **385.** Amethyst Carnival Greengard Furniture Co. advertising plate (note the "double handgrip" shape). **386.** Amethyst Carnival Pipe Humidor. **387.** Amethyst Carnival Dolphin compote with Rosalind interior (see also Fig. 378). **388.** Amethyst Carnival Court House bowl ("unlettered" version) with three-in-one edge. **389.** Marigold Carnival Pipe Humidor. **390.** Amethyst Carnival Court House bowl (6 5/8" d., 2 1/8" high; collectors call this the "cereal bowl" to differentiate it from the round, but flatter ice cream bowl). **391.** Amethyst Carnival Cleveland Memorial ashtray. **392.** Marigold Carnival Hobstar and Feather diamond-shaped piece from Bridge Set. **393.** Amethyst Carnival Isaac Benesch advertising ruffled bowl. **394.** Marigold Carnival whimsey made from Feather and Heart tumbler. **395.** Lavender Carnival Court House ruffled bowl.

page 134
396. Green Carnival Hobstar and Feather punch bowl with base (the base is actually marigold Carnival to which green paint has been added). **397.** Green Carnival Hobstar and Feather punch cup.

page 135
398. Amethyst Carnival Big Thistle punch bowl. **399.** Green Carnival Diamonds punch bowl. **400.** Amethyst Carnival Multi-Fruits and Flowers punch bowl and base. **401.** Blue Carnival Multi-Fruits and Flowers punch cup.

page 136
402. Crystal opalescent Country Kitchen bowl. **403.** Crystal opalescent Country Kitchen crimped bowl. **404.** Amethyst Carnival Grape Leaves bowl and another view which shows the Mayflower back. **405-408.** Marigold Carnival Country Kitchen table set—spooner, covered sugar bowl, covered butterdish and creamer.

page 137
409. Marigold Carnival Diamonds punch bowl and base. **410.** Vaseline Carnival Many Stars square bowl. **411.** Vaseline Carnival Peacock banana boat-shaped bowl. **412.** Vaseline Carnival Strawberry Wreath compote (note the incomplete, unfinished leaf)

page 138

413. This extraordinary Nesting Swan bowl was discovered in an Oregon shop in the summer of 1994. The interesting Marigold Carnival iridescence was not produced by the usual method, i. e., spraying hot glass. This piece should be called "Lustred ware," and its beauty certainly ranks with Carnival glass. After it was pressed and shaped, this crystal bowl was cooled to room temperature. Then, solutions of metallic salts were applied with a brush, and the bowl was placed in a decorating lehr to create the iridescent finish. **414-415.** Green Carnival Morning Glory tumbler and pitcher. **416.** This tall blown vase is certainly a one-of-a-kind Millersburg piece. It now resides in the Fenton Museum in Williamstown, West Virginia. The museum obtained the vase through descendents of H. W. Stanley, a Marietta businessman who was an early investor in John W. Fenton's Millersburg venture. The vase, which has a pontil mark, was blown off-hand (no mould was used). While still hot, the vase was stuck-up to be shaped and then sprayed with a metallic salt solution to produce the light marigold iridescent finish.

page 139

417. Amethyst Carnival Elk bowl. **418.** Marigold Carnival Blackberry Wreath Variant 9" bowl. **419.** Amethyst Carnival Blackberry Wreath chop plate. **420.** Amethyst Carnival Elk paperweight

page 140

421. People's Vase in blue Carnival. **422.** People's Vase in green Carnival **423.** People's Vase in amethyst (note ruffled top) Carnival.

page 141

424. Marigold Carnival People's Vase (11 1/4" tall) showing the details on all areas of the vase.

page 142

425. Amethyst Carnival Mitered Ovals vase. **426.** Amethyst Carnival Hanging Cherries banana boat whimsey made from compote **427.** Marigold Carnival Hobstar and Feather heart-shaped piece from Bridge Set. **428.** Amethyst Carnival "Campbell Beesley Co. Spring Opening 1911" advertising plate (note "handgrip"). **429.** Amethyst Carnival Gay Nineties tumbler. **430.** Amethyst Carnival Gay Nineties pitcher. **431.** Unusual green opalescent Ohio Star vase.

page 143

432. Blue Ohio Star compote (not iridized). **433.** Amethyst Swirl Hobnail spittoon (not iridized).

page 144

434-436. Hobstar and Feather compotes; the bowls are somewhat different shapes, and Figs. 434 and 436 have frosted leaves. **437-438.** Hobstar and Feather tumbler and pitcher with frosted leaves. **439.** Hobstar and Feather 4" x 8" applesauce boat . **440.** Hobstar and Feather 7" x 5" pickle dish. **441.** Hobstar and Feather flat sauce dish or small plate, 6" d. **442-443.** Hobstar and Feather stemmed rose bowls with frosted leaves (note the different shapes of the bowls; Fig. 442 measures 2" at the opening). The pieces in the bottom row were long thought to be Millersburg's Diamonds pattern. They are not Millersburg glass, as explained in this book (see pp. 19-20). The sugar bowl base, creamer and butterdish with ruby-stain decoration and the crystal tumbler were made by the Tarentum Glass Company, c. 1898. The toothpick holder with ruby flash and gold lettering ("Millersburg Carnival Glass. Millersburg, Ohio Founded 1909") is not old; these were made as souvenirs by the Guernsey Glass Co. in the early 1970s.

page 145

444. Ohio Star ice cream bowl. **445.** Hobstar and Feather ice cream bowl. **446.** Ohio Star vase. **447.** Hobstar and Feather 8" x 11" banana boat. **448.** Ohio Star stemmed rose bowl. **449.** Hobstar and Feather whimsey tray. **450-451.** Hobstar and Feather ice cream sauce dishes, one has collar base other has a flat bottom. **452.** Palm Wreath oval-shaped creamer. **453.** Palm Wreath cruet. **454.** Ohio Star cider tumbler. **455-456.** Ohio Star punch cups, slightly different sizes. **457.** Ohio Star toothpick holder. **458.** Hobstar and Feather sherbet dish 4" tall, 3 7/8" d.

page 146
459-462. Ohio Star table set—butterdish, sugar bowl, spooner and creamer. **463.** Marilyn pitcher. **464.** Country Kitchen ice cream bowl (note the turned in edge). **465.** Country Kitchen 6" ruffled sauce dish. **466.** Country Kitchen 6" sauce dish with turned-in edge, almost like a rose bowl. **467.** Country Kitchen ice cream bowl (very shallow, without turned-in edge). **468.** Cactus 9" bowl, plain interior. **469.** Feather and Heart pitcher. **470.** Fine Cut Heart 9" bowl, plain interior.

page 147
471. Hobstar and Feather punch bowl with base. **472.** Hobstar and Feather punch cups (note the frosted leaves on all of these pieces).

BIBLIOGRAPHY

Butler Brothers catalogs, titled "Our Drummer," various issues (cited in text or photo credits), 1910-1912

"Dog Dishes and Targets Are Collectible Antiques," *Holmes County Farmer-Hub*, July 17, 1975 (this article may have been written by George Irving).

Edwards, Bill. *Millersburg, The Queen of Carnival Glass*. Paducah, KY: Collector Books, 1975.

Edwards, Bill. *Millersburg Crystal Glassware*. Paducah, KY: Collector Books,1982.

Edwards, Bill. *Standard Encyclopedia of Carnival Glass*, 4th ed. Paducah, KY: Collector Books, 1994.

Hartung, Marion T. "Carnival Glass Series," 1-10.

Heacock, William. *Fenton Glass: The First Twenty-five Years*. Marietta, Ohio: O-Val Advertising Corp., 1978.

HOACGA Notebook Series, Pitchers and Table Sets.

Irving, George. "The Millersburg Glass Story," in 9th Annual Holmes County Antique Festival Souvenir program (1971).

Irving, George. "The Glass Era of Millersburg - Part II," in 10th Annual Holmes County Antique Festival Souvenir program (1972).

Lincoln-Land Newsletters 1977-1994.

Lowe, Lucille. "Rise and fall of the Millersburg Glass Company left heritage and claim to fame never thought possible," *Holmes County Farmer-Hub*, special edition, October 8, 1987.

Moore, Donald E. *The Shape of Things in Carnival Glass*. Alameda, CA: 1975

Moore, Donald E. *The Complete Guide to Carnival Glass Rarities*. Alameda, CA: by author, ND.

Mordini, Tom and Sharon. *Carnival Glass Auction Price Report*. Issued yearly by the authors from 36 N. Mernitz Ave., Freeport, IL 61032 ($9.00 postpaid).

Resnik, John D. *The Encyclopedia of Carnival Glass Lettered Pieces*. Nevada City, CA: by author, 1989.

Wilson, Jack D. *Millersburg Research Notes*. 1982.

Millersburg Glass: As I know It
by Marie McGee

1995-96 Value Guide

During the past several years, the popularity and demand for Millersburg Carnival Glass have caused prices to change rapidly, with the value of many examples soaring upward. This makes it difficult to determine accurate market values. Condition, color, iridescence and availability determine what a collector will pay.

The prices given here reflect public auctions as well as private sales and consultations with collectors. For some extraordinarily rare items, no price (NP) is indicated because the item has not changed hands for many years (some Millersburg items—such as unusual variations, whimseys and other rare items—seldom change hands).

Neither the author or the publishers can be liable for any losses incurred when using this guide as the basis for any transaction.

#	Value	#	Value	#	Value	#	Value
1	100	28	1100	55	125	82	375
2	200	29	800	56	4100	83	1000
3	75	30	2000	57	600	84	600
4	95	31	250	58	325	85	40
5	1900	32	50	59	295	86	35
6	800	33	200	60	450	87	2500
7	1400	34	250	61	400	88	1000
8	450	35	160	62	350	89	5000
9	70	36	300	63	350	90	2500
10	3200	37	200	64	9000	91	1000
11	160	38	90	65	1150	92	700
12	100	39	90	66	95	93	200
13	60	40	300	67	170	94	125
14	120	41	300	68	125	95	195
15	80	42	125	69	295	96	135
16	125	43	2000	70	100	97	210
17	200	44	2500	71	115	98	60
18	200	45	9900	72	100	99	175
19	220	46	140	73	850	100	3000
20	180	47	90	74	165	101	75
21	2600	48	185	75	NP	102	125
22	15000	49	65	76	1450	103	95
23	2100	50	6000	77	3000	104	2400
24	NP	51	75	78	3000	105	90
25	1200	52	210	79	1200	106	210
26	700	53	75	80	2500	107	75
27	275	54	1000	81	1800	108	NP

109	-	200	163	-	15000	217	-	1200	271	-	NP
110	-	135	164	-	9000	218	-	3300	272	-	NP
111	-	400	165	-	300	219	-	3000	273	-	NP
112	-	180	166	-	500	220	-	3300	274	-	NP
113	-	120	167	-	300	221	-	10000	275	-	NP
114	-	400	168	-	1000	222	-	7000	276	-	2000
115	-	135	169	-	400	223	-	500	277	-	2250
116	-	135	170	-	600	224	-	400	278	-	2500
117	-	130	171	-	2250	225	-	350	279	-	400
118	-	435	172	-	1950	226	-	250	280	-	14000
119	-	400	173	-	1900	227	-	400	281	-	900
120	-	2500	174	-	450	228	-	600	282	-	1150
121	-	200	175	-	525	229	-	500	283	-	6100
122	-	475	176	-	350	230	-	250	284	-	1200
123	-	325	177	-	550	231	-	1800	285	-	1300
124	-	1000	178	-	600	232	-	1000	286	-	375
125	-	1200	179	-	550	233	-	600	287	-	100
126	-	NP	180	-	75	234	-	NP	288	-	1000
127	-	400	181	-	80	235	-	1400	289	-	2600
128	-	650	182	-	90	236	-	500	290	-	2100
129	-	500	183	-	400	237	-	1100	291	-	2400
130	-	400	184	-	6500	238	-	350	292	-	4250
131	-	125	185	-	410	239	-	350	293	-	400
132	-	90	186	-	310	240	-	600	294	-	140
133	-	225	187	-	210	241	-	NP	295	-	800
134	-	1000	188	-	130	242	-	400	296	-	2250
135	-	800	189	-	165	243	-	9900	297	-	2250
136	-	1000	190	-	500	244	-	700	298	-	500
137	-	1500	191	-	550	245	-	400	299	-	495
138	-	1450	192	-	1100	246	-	395	300	-	400
139	-	1250	193	-	1600	247	-	150	301	-	2400
140	-	2600	194	-	3100	248	-	1000	302	-	800
141	-	325	195	-	350	249	-	600	303	-	675
142	-	195	196	-	400	250	-	2250	304	-	850
143	-	500	197	-	2400	251	-	800	305	-	300
144	-	11000	198	-	7200	252	-	800	306	-	160
145	-	1200	199	-	2600	253	-	5000	307	-	375
146	-	2100	200	-	425	254	-	250	308	-	950
147	-	2700	201	-	225	255	-	250	309	-	2200
148	-	2200	202	-	550	256	-	175	310	-	1200
149	-	1600	203	-	200	257	-	150	311	-	4000
150	-	600	204	-	250	258	-	950	312	-	325
151	-	400	205	-	95	259	-	NP	313	-	400
152	-	200	206	-	2000	260	-	1200	314	-	3200
153	-	1000	207	-	1200	261	-	3000	315	-	2900
154	-	350	208	-	250	262	-	7500	316	-	1450
155	-	350	209	-	1800	263	-	3500	317	-	400
156	-	500	210	-	175	264	-	1800	318	-	850
157	-	800	211	-	475	265	-	NP	319	-	4600
158	-	1200	212	-	250	266	-	NP	320	-	3000
159	-	500	213	-	375	267	-	NP	321	-	1500
160	-	250	214	-	350	268	-	NP	322	-	1200
161	-	600	215	-	575	269	-	NP	323	-	1200
162	-	350	216	-	2800	270	-	NP	324	-	850

325	-	550	362	-	950	399	-	2000	436	-	75
326	-	1300	363	-	125	400	-	8500	437	-	75
327	-	180	364	-	750	401	-	2000	438	-	275
328	-	3200	365	-	495	402	-	125	439	-	55
329	-	575	366	-	1200	403	-	150	440	-	40
330	-	875	367	-	500	404	-	750	441	-	65
331	-	2200	368	-	175	405	-	350	442	-	200
332	-	400	369	-	1800	406	-	200	443	-	150
333	-	1300	370	-	200	407	-	400	444	-	50
334	-	400	371	-	1500	408	-	170	445	-	50
335	-	450	372	-	275	409	-	5500	446	-	75
336	-	250	373	-	8000	410	-	13000	447	-	150
337	-	3000	374	-	8500	411	-	NP	448	-	180
338	-	290	375	-	2000	412	-	2100	449	-	40
339	-	260	376	-	250	413	-	600	450	-	35
340	-	900	377	-	1600	414	-	1000	451	-	35
341	-	850	378	-	2650	415	-	15500	452	-	60
342	-	600	379	-	13000	416	-	NP	453	-	70
343	-	1500	380	-	NP	417	-	1800	454	-	45
344	-	800	381	-	2000	418	-	250	455	-	22
345	-	400	382	-	1200	419	-	NP	456	-	25
346	-	1650	383	-	NP	420	-	850	457	-	75
347	-	4100	384	-	700	421	-	35000	458	-	45
348	-	1400	385	-	1600	422	-	35000	459	-	60
349	-	600	386	-	7500	423	-	25000	460	-	50
350	-	450	387	-	2650	424	-	35000	461	-	30
351	-	425	388	-	2400	425	-	7000	462	-	30
352	-	1300	389	-	5000	426	-	NP	463	-	85
353	-	1300	390	-	1200	427	-	350	464	-	100
354	-	13500	391	-	8000	428	-	1400	465	-	20
355	-	1250	392	-	300	429	-	1000	466	-	40
356	-	3500	393	-	450	430	-	10000	467	-	45
357	-	1000	394	-	6000	431	-	25000	468	-	45
358	-	300	395	-	1200	432	-	NP	469	-	145
359	-	1200	396	-	3000	433	-	NP	470	-	50
360	-	1000	397	-	65	434	-	100	471	-	750
361	-	12500	398	-	10000	435	-	75	472	-	35

FRONT COVER

A 1000 Green Carnival Many Stars ice cream bowl (note radium finish).

B 350 Marigold Carnival Strawberry Wreath ice cream bowl.

C 1000 Amethyst Carnival Millersburg Court House 7" ice cream shape bowl (note radium finish).

D 1000 Amethyst Carnival Swirl Hobnail spittoon.

E 1000 Blue Carnival Millersburg Peacock 6" ruffled sauce dish.

BACK COVER

F 1800 Green Carnival Hobstar and Feather rose bowl.

G 8000 Amethyst Carnival Cleveland Memorial ashtray.

H 2250 Vaseline Carnival Whirling Leaves square bowl.

I 250 Amethyst Carnival Strawberry Wreath 6" flat sauce dish.

J 2700 Amethyst Carnival Peacock ice cream bowl.

K 5000 Blue Carnival Vintage 10" bowl with Hobnail back.